# MY LIFE AMONG THE GENTILES

*To Chuck —*
*You and your*
*suggestions!*

# My Life Among
## the Gentiles

*Shalom*

**by** *Miriam*

**MIRIAM NEWELL BISKIN**

Authors Choice Press
New York   Bloomington

# My Life Among the Gentiles

Authors Choice Press
an imprint of iUniverse

iUniverse books may be ordered through booksellers or by contacting:

iUniverse
1663 Liberty Drive
Bloomington, IN 47403
www.iuniverse.com
1-800-Authors (1-800-288-4677)

ISBN: 978-1-4401-7404-9 (pbk)

Printed in the United States of America

iUniverse rev. date: 2/11/10

*To my beloved more-than-better half*

# Preface

A word to the reader:

These stories are a part of my life as I see it. The people mentioned are composites of many personalities and most of the names are fictitious. Therefore, I suggest that you refrain from trying to seek out identities. My humble purpose is to enlighten and amuse, nothing more.

# Contents

## Contents

MY LIFE AMONG THE GENTILES

# 1  I Find Out

I don't recall the exact date of that red-letter day, but I have a hazy recollection that it was about the same time I learned that I was a Democrat and not a Republican, poor instead of rich, and that there was a host of other unrelated facts concerning inherited characteristics. I must have asked the proverbial question, "What am I?" and received the proverbial answer, "If anyone asks you, just say you're-a-Jew-and-proud-of-it." In this manner, I became hyphenated Hebrew—with the idea gradually seeping into my childish mentality that everyone was not of the *genus Judicius* and that somehow I had a position to maintain.

If I had any questions about why I should be so defensively proud, I didn't ask them, but simply absorbed my mother's words; because if she said something was so, it was. I did feel some vague uneasiness, for instinct told me that if I was to be on the defensive, there must be an aggressor close by.

Hostile enemies had not as yet troubled me personally,

but tales of their conduct hovered in the air like so many dark and threatening clouds. My brothers had been chased home from school by boys who yelled "sheeney" and "kike," and I knew that these boys were not Jewish and that they were bigger and that there were more of them.

Many times at night as I lay in my bed I could hear my mother and father's voices from the kitchen. Papa would sip his glass of tea as he listened to Mama tell stories about the old country. I shivered in the darkness at her reminiscences of the *pogroms*: of the villages fired by marauding Cossacks; of the taking of small Jewish boys to serve in the Czar's army, for so many years away from family and home that they forget their heritage completely.

It was as real to me as if I had been there—that horrible night when a Polish neighbor, a baker, had actually hidden the Jewish children in his huge ovens hoping that the Cossacks would not be clever enough to find them in such an odd hiding place. As I drifted off into restless sleep, I could hear the clip-clop of the horses' hooves moving off into the night and I hardly dared breathe.

But this was America, far away from the flaming nationalistic hatreds of nineteenth-century Russia and Poland, far from pogroms and fanatic anti-Semitism—twentieth century America was the reality of my small waking life, quite apart from that subconscious crammed full of the dark fears and the darker angers of prenatal memory.

I was the last of the litter, so that by the time I entered school the community had grown more or less used to having us around. Our difference was accepted and a few friendships had begun to blossom.

But somehow there remained a feeling of being an outsider, of not really belonging; for a Northern mill town can be as incestuously clannish as any Southern center of aristocracy, as generation after generation of inbreeding produces a musty code of morality, shaped and qualified by convenience and clan loyalty. Hatreds lie murky and hidden until clashes for power bring them out—violent and vicious.

What was it like—this city of shadows and memories and baby days? Old, not graciously and proudly ancient with its long American lineage; but simply tired and crackled and worn by the weight of passing years; tired like the cobbled towns of Europe where small brick houses stand shoulder to shoulder, row on row; and where dark and polluted air makes a heavy low ceiling. Few people had any real comprehension of the past, any pride in the present, or any dream for the future. Here was a place that might have been, where hopes were promising green grapes too soon gnawed away by the foxes of self-interest and self-deception.

We lived in an upended rectangle of a house trisected horizontally by three parallel porches that made the front of its grey frame structure topheavy. The inside architecture featured great length and its only advantage was room —two parlors, a dining room, four bedrooms, a kitchen; and a huge glassed-in rear addition called a summer kitchen. There were closets and porches, a cellar and an attic and a big backyard. We lived in the first floor flat and rented out the upper two.

The backyard was my playground and my mother's garden—a motley collection of blue morning glories, yellow marigolds and variegated petunias. In the spring, there was the heavy fragrance of purple lilacs, and in the fall, the sweet aroma of red grapes on the arbor. But every hour of every day, the soft fragrances and the bright colors

were overlaid by the soot and smoke of the trains that
chugged by on the tracks just behind our house.

Our front yard terraced down to a cobbled road bi-
sected by trolley tracks; on the other side of the street were
rows of small houses perched on the side of the old Erie
Canal. The frontyard and the backyard were my playgrounds and my prisons; for I was forbidden to go beyond
their confines. I played princess pretending that the canal
was my moat and the railroad track the boundary line of
the property of a bewitched Benares—a smoking monster
that would transport me to dark places if it chose.

Up the street and down the street and on the next street
were our town's ghettos, whose charming names still in-
trude themselves in memory. Down the road and across
the canal was Sheeney Town where most of the town's
Jewish population lived. Our family—a trifle more middle-
class—had made its exodus across the bridge from this
circumscribed area but returned regularly for comfortable camaraderie. Those financially better-off moved further away, literally and spiritually.

Two blocks above our interim position was Skunk Hol-
low, the home of the Poles and Ukrainians and Russians
who had been imported to work in the cotton mills. Their
huge double-domed cathedral presided over a cluster of
small crowded homes. On the banks of the Dneiper, its
lavish rococo style would have been fitting; on the shores
of the Hudson, it was unexpected.

Main Street was not the main street and ran above and
parallel to the railroad track—not dividing the rich and
poor, only separating the poor from each other. This area
was little Italy, where Sicilians and Italians perpetuated
old vendettas and where outsiders treaded softly, frightened by tales about the Mafia and the Black Hand.

There were many Canadian-French inhabitants, affectionately referred to as "Canucks" and "frogs" by their cosmopolitan neighbors. These people clung loyally to their native tongue and translated their bit of culture to this bit of American soil.

No town on the banks of the Erie Canal would be complete without its own "Limerick" where the "shanty Irish" and the "lace-curtain Irish" practiced a less-than-peaceful coexistence with a social structure based on the most exacting protocol, for those who had certain jobs on the canals were considered better than others. With the English, their snobbery was similar, since those with certain jobs in the mills felt superior to people who held other more menial positions. Eventually as the daughters of the canal-working Irish married the sons of the mill-working English, the vitality of their breed all but obliterated the lesser strain; and the children of these unions became devout Catholics and devoted Irishmen. The only clue to their other progenitors was a Puritan attitude that would have been at home in Massachusetts Bay. Tradition was overlaid upon tradition until the community became a veritable melting pot where the only thing many residents had in common was the pot.

Second and third generations were all-Americans and abandoned the old languages and cultures; but they retained the item closest to the hearts—intolerance for each other. The fourth and fifth generations moved neither backward nor forward—they just stagnated.

But amid echoes and shadows and animosities, our home was a warm sanctuary presided over by my parents, where Mama's baking and cooking filled the house with sweet fragrant smells, and Papa kept us all safe. Friday was the most wonderful day. The greyest of grey moods brightened as I came home from school and opened the kitchen door to be greeted by the magic *Erev Shabbos* aroma of a giant pot of chicken soup lavishly flavored with parsley and celery and carrots—the pans full of sweet raisin and cinnamon buns and the row upon row of golden braided challahs. . . .

To Mama, braiding challah was an art, and she loved to show us all the patterns into which she could arrange the long strips of dough, each carrying its own special meaning. She made her dough long before we awoke in the morning and placed it in great towel-covered bowlfuls on the kitchen radiators to rise. When it had expanded sufficiently, she would knead with her strong hands and then begin to braid the loaves.

The first step for a *frumë balubusta* was a bit of ritual. She would stand over the big black cast-iron stove, lift one of the round lids, and as the dough spattered on the bright coals, say the words of thanksgiving for all that God had given us and pray that no one in the world would go without bread. She would always set aside dough to be made into extra loaves for neighbors who were sick or needy, or just old and lonely and often forgotten.

Then the ceremony of braiding began. Pieces of dough rolled into long strips were arranged in groups of three or four or five, depending on Mama's whim. Pinching the strips together at one end, she would then bind them into a pattern of intricate convolutions. Holiday loaves were the only ones not braided—these she made by stacking the dough layer upon layer. As a final touch, she would dip a long white chicken feather into a bowl of beaten egg yolk and gild the top of each loaf with an artistic flourish: this last operation gave the *challah* a shiny yellow glaze.

The smell of baking bread unofficially announced the coming of *Shabbos*. The official pronouncement came after Mama had swept the kitchen and had set the supper table with a clean white cloth. Then, placing a small shawl on her head, she would light the *Shabbos* candles and intone a prayer of thanks to God for his blessings. Standing with hands clasped, her body swaying, her eyes filled with tears I could not comprehend, she would chant the ancient Hebrew words; and as the candles flickered and the words of blessing filled the warm kitchen, I knew who I was and where I belonged.

# 2  Chicken Soup

My mother's creative passions impelled her to make all sorts of calorie-laden concoctions for her captive audience of eaters—her family. She made mounds of *kugel* and pans of nut-filled *strudel*. And we consumed every last crumb. We also gorged ourselves on such minor taste treats as rye bread crusts covered with chicken *schmaltz* and rubbed in with union or garlic. The angel who guards over cases of heartburn must have been kept busy watching over us.

On Friday nights, the menu was traditionally constant —baked chicken preceded by chicken soup which my mother served in plates that had the same volume as a small *vana* (bathtub). I was the youngest child, the most defenseless, but my portions were exactly as large as those of my three elder brothers—and my eating capabilities were judged in comparison to theirs. Only by the most gargantuan efforts could I manage to consume the huge plate of soup with noodles and the enormous platter of chicken and potatoes and vegetables that was set before me. If I left even the tiniest morsel, I would be greeted by heavy maternal sighs and a line which was always the same.

*"Ach, mein fegele—ze est gurnit."* ("Oh, my little bird—she eats nothing.")

Years later when my skinny frame finally made the reckoning for years of overeating and I was driven to diets, my mother would still maintain that I had the appetite of a bird, and my husband would mutter in tones that only I could overhear, "Yeah—a vulture."

My mother had a thing about chicken soup. She was sure of its medicinal qualities and used it in lieu of aspirin, penicillin and sulfa. Positive that it aided physical and mental growth, she also used it as a substitute for vitamin pills. Taken internally, it could cure hangnails and sore muscles. Not to partake of this delicacy on any and all occasions brought dire predictions of gloom and disaster ranging from threats of a poor complexion to the danger of having one's growth stunted.

So on each and every Friday, she made gallons of this golden concoction and added celery and parsley and homemade noodles to a point where it was no longer drinkable or even easily edible. And I knew that even after finishing this one-dish meal, I would still be expected to make my way through the main course. Vainly, I battled the inevitable.

"No soup tonight, Ma."

"No soup? Who ever heard of such a thing?"

"Not so much, Ma."

"It's not much."

"Ma—no noodles, Ma!"

"Just a few."

It was a losing fight, but I kept trying. Somewhere in

my late teens I was emancipated, and my mother was sure I would grow emaciated, but I was just too old to be cajoled or bullied any longer.

To this day, I rarely eat soup. It's not that I dislike the stuff—it's just that I reached my saturation point long years ago. My husband and children complain that I don't make soup like Grandma does, but it just never occurs to me as a menu possibility.

One day I listened to the conversation as my mother ladled out her golden brew to my offspring.

"Hey, Grandma, aren't you going to eat with us?"

"I never eat when I serve. You eat—I'll eat later."

The children accepted her dictum just as we always had and attacked their noodles with glee. Grandma sat down beside me.

"You won't have something to eat, *fegele?*"

"No, Mom—I'm cutting down. How about you? Aren't you having something?"

"I'm not hungry now."

"Mom," I said, thinking back, "I don't ever remember seeing you have a bowl of chicken soup. I've seen you make it and serve it but I've never seen you eat it."

"Chicken soup?" she said, mouthing the two words and then whispering carefully so that the children couldn't hear, "Chicken soup—I never eat chicken soup. I hate chicken soup!"

# 3  Grey Loom the Ghosts

My town was a mill town, and the Industrial Revolution that changed the face of America had changed my town's face too. Where once Dutch patroons had looked out over placid green fields and rolling hills, English textile manufacturers had constructed an exact replica of a cobbled British mill town complete with long rows of factories from whose chimneys rose black clouds to replace the tumbling mists of waterfalls. There was no prevention to man's invention, and by 1900 poets ceased to marvel at the beauty of the valley, for there was little left to marvel at.

It was as though old Manchester or Liverpool had been transported and dropped in the center of Eden—complete with soot and cinders. Railroad tracks crisscrossed the streets of the town, the builders oblivious to both safety and appearance in their anxiety to set up proper transportation to haul away the bounty that had been produced by harnessed water power.

The population, too, was the result of the growth of the mills. Whole towns were imported first from England and then from Eastern and Southern Europe to provide the labor force for the new factories. This all happened many years before I was born and yet I can remember riding up past the mills in our Model T. My father would always point to one long building and say, "That's where I went to work when I was just nine years old."

My own seven-year-old eyes would widen in wonder. The mill with its narrow blue-tinted windows looked menacing, and I felt as though someone might rush out through the wide wooden doors and drag me inside and chain me to a machine. I would snuggle deeper into my grey wool chinchilla coat and hug my muff tightly. I would look down at my shining, high-button, patent leather shoes: twin beacons in my own secure comfortable world.

"How could you work, Daddy?" I would ask. "You were only a little boy."

"Many little boys and little girls worked. They gave me a box to stand on so I could reach a bobbin and keep the thread straight."

"But when did you play?"

"I didn't. At least I don't remember playing. It was dark when I went to work and dark when I came home."

"But how could you go to school?"

"I didn't go to school. When I was older—in fact, after I was married—I went to night school to learn to read and write."

"Didn't your Mommy mind?"

"She minded, but we needed the money. We had a big family to feed."

"Didn't anybody mind?"

"Oh, there were some laws against children working . . .

especially boys my size. But when the mill inspector would come, the men would hide me inside my box and slide it to the other end of the floor. As soon as he left, they would slide me back."

I never grew tired of asking the same questions over and over and getting the same answers. He would tell me how the cotton was made into thread and the thread into knit goods and the knit goods into long underwear—and how that long underwear was sent all over the country; all over the world.

I listened carefully, but I couldn't imagine my father as a little boy. In time, the continued recitation of this autobiographical catechism produced a child who lived a shadowy existence in my life, quite apart from both of us. This child stood on a box close to a big machine as if he were under an enchanted spell that would never let him free. His sad eyes would look at me and at my shiny patent leather shoes, but he never came to take my hand or ask me to run and play. When I smiled, he did not seem to see . . . he simply turned his head back to the machine . . . and then the long red-brick walls would close him out of my sight.

Behind the walls of another mill near the levees of the Mississippi was another child who had been left there when my mother grew up to be my mother. Methodically rolling cigars, she sat at a table with her dark brown eyes intent upon the broad leaves that stained her fingers. The perspiration ran down the back of her dress, and her black-stockinged legs ached from being in one position so long—but she never looked up from her work. I knew she saw my chinchilla coat and my muff, but she appeared not to notice me at all.

These two children had come so far; they had survived

the searching lashes of the Cossacks, the murderous venom of the *pogroms,* the freezing journey across the ocean. I could see them, two little immigrants with only the bundles of rags they called their possessions to sleep on. And now they were here where there were green meadows full of white daisies and yellow black-eyed susans and where the air was warm and free—yet they did not dance or sing.

Mama and Papa were grownups with a business and a family and a home—people who stood tall and raised their children in the tradition of this land of plenty. They could buy good food and warm clothes and too many toys. But perhaps one doll was meant for that little girl with the tobacco-stained fingers and one rocking horse for the little boy standing on a box by the loom. In my memory, I can still see those grey waifs somberly staring at me through the mists of the past—they stare at my shoes and my toys, but they do not smile.

# 4  Grandma and the Confederacy*

I always think of Grandmother Hannah as a lady in a
*sheitel*. That's what always fascinated me about her picture—that *sheitel* and the old-fashioned blouse with the
tucked bodice and the leg-of-mutton sleeves. This was the
picture of a prim and genteel Jewish lady—hardly the type
that you would expect to be mixed up in a money swindle,
and yet (may my words not be too hard on her revered
memory!), she was.

Oh, this all took place many years ago in the 1870's,
and it started in a little village to the east of Odessa. That
was where my Grandfather lived, with his family. He was
a trader, who bought horses for resale to the Czar and
searched far and wide for the best animals at the cheapest
prices. Most of the time his search took him into the area
around Constantinople—a place where a Jew might tread
fearfully but where no Christian dared enter. The horses
he bought were brought back to his farm until they could
be sold.

* Reprinted from *The Jewish Digest*

Grandpa was a handsome man, tall of stature and bearded of face. His bright eyes were like summer skies and a song hung forever upon his lips. At every wedding, his fine voice and his fiddle were in demand. The young men and the girls loved to dance to his music; the old men laughed at his stories. The women, eyeing him closely, were jealous that Grandma should have such a man.

Grandma had the tiny figure of a girl. She did not look like the mother of many children, but she was; and she ruled them like a martinet. In fact, that was just about the way she ruled Grandpa, too. A devout woman—she loved God, her husband and her children in that order—she might complain about her husband or her children, but never would she say a word that questioned the will of the Almighty.

Grandpa was not so traditional. In fact, there was one large area where he did not see eye to eye with the Lord. This was in the matter of children. Grandpa felt that the Lord had been more than cooperative and generous in the provision of offspring, and he planned to thwart the divine scheme which added an annual baby to his home. Grandma shrugged off his crazy ideas. Whatever the Lord provided, she accepted; and that included babies. In her strict, unsentimental way, she welcomed them into a strict and unsentimental world. Grandpa, however, was bent on his experiment in planned parenthood, and after great deliberation he announced that he would guarantee abstinence by staying away for at least twelve months.

"This year," he boasted, "no babies."

Stoically, he bore the discomfitures of the poor facilities of the Russian inns. Wandering farther north than he had ever been before, putting miles between himself and connubial bliss, he suffered all the torments of his enforced bachelorhood. His only consolation was the thought of his hard-won victory. Finally, the year passed and he returned home. Nine months later, however, his well-plotted triumph became an ashen defeat as Grandma presented him with a set of twins.

"See, Mendel," said Grandma, "it is God's will. The baby we did not have last year, the Lord saved for us for this year." For this was her firm belief. Grandma was always proud of her understanding of God's will and sometimes even prouder of her husband's virility.

"All my Mendel has to do is hang his pants in our bedroom and I am with child." Grandpa had no choice but to surrender to the inevitabilities of life and these inevitabilities eventually numbered ten.

Grandma's children were treated like adults from the moment they could walk; they fed the chickens and milked the cows; they brushed the horses and cleaned the barns. Work was never-ending on the farm, and worse than the work was the feeling of constant apprehension. Two miles from the nearest neighbor, they were at the mercy of weather and loneliness and marauding Cossacks. Usually, Grandpa's property was left untouched because of his dealings with the commissar of the armies, but when these men were drunk, their discretion could not be counted upon. Their natural inbred hatred of the Jews could become an incendiary passion that could easily put any property to the torch.

Thus it was that one night before Easter the Cossacks raged drunkenly over the countryside. One of Grandma's neighbors came to warn her and bundled the whole family into his hay wagon and hid them under an old bridge all night. In the chill dampness, the poor children huddled together too terrified to sleep. By morning, nothing was left. The barns, the house, the fields had been burned; the animals had been driven off or stolen.

To this charred wreckage, Grandpa returned. He cared for nothing, however, except his family. Over and over, he caressed each child's face and thanked God for each one's safety.

"Hannah, we must leave this place. We cannot stay here."

"Where—where can we go?"

"To America—there one may live in peace."

"But, Mendel, we have not the money to take all of us to America. How could such a thing ever be?" Grandma was too discouraged to even share Grandpa's dream.

"We have enough for one, and I shall go. I will work hard and send you money. Then you will be able to come to America with all the children."

"Then we shall be able to live in a country without fear."

Carefully, they made their plans. Grandpa was to go off to America to make his fortune, and Grandma was to stay behind with their brood at the home of Uncle Shimin. As soon as he was able, Grandpa would send for them.

Grandpa landed in New York with high hopes and no cash. Relatives took him in, made a bed for him on the couch, and found him a job in a tailor shop. He lugged boxes and swept floors and learned the rudiments of tailoring. In the process, he learned a little English and a little of the ways of the New World. His loneliness for his family drove him to thinking constantly of ways to make money. There was money to be made if one just knew how . . . he watched the pushcart peddlers and a wish for a business of his own grew in his heart.

Little by little, penny by penny, he saved to buy his

pushcart. In his mind, it became a magic carpet that would transport his family across the sea. The great day finally arrived when he was able to display his wares on Delancey Street. No one sent him a basket of flowers to wish him luck at his grand opening; no one even noticed him in the hurly-burly and the push; but he was a happy man.

He continued to work and to save, but there was never quite enough in that little sack that he had sewed inside the lining of his overcoat. New York was a lonely dirty place, and he yearned to see green fields and meadows and to breathe the sweet smell of fresh air.

Perhaps if he had a horse and buggy, he could carry on his trade that way. In other places, business was less competitive and he could make money faster. Hannah and the children would be able to come to America even sooner. So he bought a horse and buggy! Not much of a horse, just a scrawny bag of bones named Clancy who had spent his life drawing a brewery cart. The buggy was a replica of the wonderful one-horse shay, patched and rusty and hung together in a miraculously still-serviceable fashion.

And off Grandpa went, creaking his itinerant way south with the swallows, past Philadelphia, past Baltimore, past Atlanta into the deep South. His new customers knew little of Jews other than what they had read in the Bible, and the tall seller of housewares looked to them like one of the old prophets incarnate. They listened with awe to his singsong sales pitch and bought as though his pots and pans had been dipped in the holy River Jordan.

Grandpa's savings were growing steadily when one day he chanced to meet a magnificent gentleman, a scion of one of the wealthiest and most respected families of the Old South. This fellow wore a fancy flared grey coat and a blue brocade vest and a linen shirt with diamond studs.

Grandpa was honored that such a gentleman should ask him, a humble peddler, to share a table and a bottle of brandy. It was only at Grandpa's insistence that the gentleman allowed him to pay for the liquor. As the brandy warmed their hearts and released all the feelings of brotherhood that man holds for man, they felt impelled to share their most personal problems and to pour out all of the yearning ambitious locked so closely within them.

Grandpa told the gentleman about his farm in the old country, and the gentleman told him all about his plantation down upon the Swanee. Grandpa told him about the Cossacks and he told Grandpa about the Yankees from the North.

"*Oi vey* . . . they did to you what the Cossacks did to me. I thought such a thing could not happen in America." Grandpa was visibly shaken.

"Oh, my friend, do not worry. It is all over now. The Yankees are gone. There is nothing to fear." The gentleman's words was most reassuring and he brought forth from his carpetbag another bottle, one he had saved from those foraging scavengers, he said.

The two continued to drink and to discuss the merits of brandy and horseflesh. Each mourned the other's loss of his land, and they were soon as close as brothers.

"Mendel, I tell you—you're luckier than me. At least, you still have a family. My folks are all gone.

I am a lonely man, and it breaks my heart to think that you are separated from all that makes a man's life worth living."

"Oh, my friend, do not despair. Someday soon, I will have enough money to bring them here."

"Soon? That's not good enough. I don't want you to wait a day more and you don't have to. I can help you."

"How?"

"Well, I saved a trunkload of money from those Yankees and I'm going to give it to you. We're going to tie it up and send it off to your Hannah and tell her to buy tickets for herself and every one of those kiddies. That is what we are going to do."

"My friend, it is too much. I cannot take all that you have. This is your family fortune. You will be left penniless." Grandpa was touched by such a miraculous offer from a fellow man.

"Of course, you can take it. I've been penniless before. I'm a lone man and I need little. It will make me happy to bring you and your family together again." The stranger gulped down another brandy to steady him.

"But you must keep something so that you will not be without funds?"

"These bills can all be recognized here. I would be found and arrested if anyone here should trace them to me. I don't dare—it is too dangerous." The man's voice sank to a whisper.

"Well, then, I can help you. I have money, not a trunkload; but some money with which I can help you, my friend."

"Oh, a few dollars would be all I need to get by."

"I shall give you everything I have, just as you have given me everything." Grandpa pulled apart the stitching of his overcoat lining and forced his little bag of savings into the stranger's hand.

"Come—I will write to Hannah of our good fortune. She can get passports and soon my family will be in America."

"All right, my friend. Let us send her that letter and then I will help you to ship that trunk off to old Russia. I can just see you together with your wonderful family. You know, I don't know when I felt so good."

Grandpa wrote Grandma of their good fortune and about his generous friend who was willing to do so much for them. Grandma marveled at his wonderful tale. Such things could happen only in America.

Weeks passed and finally, the trunk arrived. She had the trucker bring it upstairs to her room, and there behind a locked and bolted door, she began to untie the ropes holding it together. Finally, she pried open the big oldfashioned lid and gasped in astonishment at the piles of bills, neatly stacked, row upon row, more paper money than she had ever seen in her life.

Busily, she and Uncle Shimin plotted a course of action. It was unthinkable to take this amount of money to a bank. There would be suspicions and questions and trouble. Instead, they would trade the money with the neighbors, and give them a generous rate of exchange in order to buy their silence. Grandma paid out ten bills to the ruble, and the butcher, the baker, and the candlestick maker traded eagerly with her. They laughed to themselves at her innocence. They knew that they were profiting over one thousand per cent on such an exchange and were perhaps momentarily conscience-stricken at taking advantage of a lowly woman, but they took the American bills and secreted them away for the day when they should visit Odessa. In a large city, at a large bank, they could make their exchange unnoticed. Happily, they counted the bonanza of rubles that would come their way.

In a matter of days, Grandma and her brood were on their way with all of their valuables packed in bundles for the long trip. Grandma clutched a pendulous beaded bag in which she had secreted a roll of precious bills for use in America when she landed. She knew that a new home needs many new things.

Grandpa was overjoyed at the sight of his wife and children. As he hugged and kissed them all, he said prayers of thanksgiving and blessed the day he had met the stranger. He led them all to their new home, a cold-water flat in a tenement on the East Side. The children could not believe their eyes. Such magnificence! Even the Czar of all the Russias did not get his water from a metal pipe in his kitchen. Over and over, they turned on the faucet and marveled at the luxury of such a convenience.

That night, after Grandpa and the children were asleep, Grandma lay awake, thinking and planning. In the morning, she would get up early and go to the shops and buy fish and cheese and fruit and cream and fix her Mendel a breakfast such as he had not had in a long time. And a tablecloth—she would buy a cloth, a white cloth. She fell asleep, content and smiling at her own dreams.

She rose early, put her shawl over her head, and went out into the still-dark street. On the corner, one little shop was already open, and Hannah was happy to find that the man spoke perfect Yiddish. She asked him for a good herring and watched as he fished one, blue and dripping, from the barrel, and packed it snugly in a piece of newspaper. He put the wrapped fish into a brown paper bag along with her sliced cheese and a few oranges. He ladled her cream into a small tin container.

"Next time you will bring me back the container, no?"

"Of course. And next time, I will remember to bring my own."

"O.K., I know how it is. Are these your first days in America?"

Grandma nodded and he began to ask her questions about the old country, where she came from, what people she knew, who she was related to and so forth. As they talked, he computed her purchases on the side of the paper bag.

"That will be fifty-three cents, please."

"Here . . ." She extracted a bill from her pendulous hoard.

He looked closely at the bill and began to shout angrily, "I can't take this!"

"Why? You can't make change? Well, I will pay you the next time I come in." Grandma turned to go.

"Thief . . . dishonest woman . . . next time? Do you think I would trust you? I am a hard-working man. Why do you try to cheat me? I have a family! Why do you try to take the bread from my children's mouths?" He pulled the paper bag from her hands.

"Cheat you? Are you crazy? I gave you money." Grandma pulled the bag back.

"Money? You call this money? That bill is Confederate. It is not worth the paper it is printed on."

With this, he pulled the bag violently, and the cheese, the herring, and the oranges broke forth and lay strewn on the floor, all bathed in a pint of sweet cream.

Well, Grandpa and the grocer eventually straightened the matter out with the aid of a policeman and a translator. Grandpa paid the grocer and learned all about the War between the States and the judgment at Appomattox. He also learned how misleading is the fact of friendship. Grandma, too, began to understand about money that has no value. But somewhere, across the ocean, across the seas, over the mountains lay a little village east of Odessa completely saturated with the currency of the Confederate States of America.

# 5  Grandpa Becomes a Citizen

From the day, Grandpa Mendel arrived in America, he was obsessed with only one idea—he wanted to become a citizen, a real part of this great and wonderful country. And as soon as it was legally possible, he took out his first papers, which was only a matter of declaring his intention to begin naturalization proceedings.

He had finally settled the family in Philadelphia and found work as a tailor. After a long day's work with the needle, he would come home to a hurried supper so that he could be off to night school. In every spare moment, he perused a small brown book entitled *English for Foreigners*. It must have been difficult for him, difficult and frustrating, but he plodded along uncomplainingly, and gradually his halting greenhorn command of English grew to fluency. At this point, he was able to enroll in Americanization classes for instruction in history and civics.

"I will make you proud of me," he would assure his children as they "heard" his recitations of the Preamble

to the Constitution, the introduction to the Declaration
of Independence and the Gettysburg Address. Never was
the Pledge of Allegiance to the flag chanted with more
sincere pride or greater vigor. With the children's aid, he
worked his way through the catechism of government
called *American Civics* and marveled at the data he de-
rived from that treasure house of information.

"A wonderful man, that Mister Lincoln," he would
muse as he intoned, " 'of the people, by the people, and
for the people.' He sounds like a Talmudist—a real
scholar."

Finally the great day came and Grandpa put on his
best suit to go to court. His hair was brushed and his
white beard glistened as he waited with his hat in his
hand, and as his honor entered, the children leaned forward across the railing so that they wouldn't miss a word.

"Mister Fishman," said His Honor, "you desire to become an American citizen?"

"Yes, sir."

"Why, Mister Fishman?"

"Because this is a great and free country where I want
to live and where I want to belong . . ."

"Very commendable, Mister Fishman. You understand
that I have to ask a few questions to test your knowledge
of this country?"

"I am ready, Your Honor." Grandpa straightened his
shoulders a little more.

"First—how deep is the Schuylkill River?"

"*Vus*—what kind of a question is that?" Grandpa
blurted out.

"You should know something about this country," the
judge countered.

"To be an American citizen, these are the things I

should know? This is more important than the Gettysburg Address?" Before the judge could reply, Grandpa dashed out of the courtroom door. His black coat tails flew out behind him, and he paused only long enough to turn and yell, "Just a minute, Your Honor!"

In a matter of seconds he reappeared with a uniformed policeman in tow. He hustled the officer up before the bench.

"Yer Honor sent for me, sir?" The man's speech was laced with heavy Irish brogue.

"No, I didn't."

"Ye didn't? Why, this lunatic of a man came runnin' out and he asked me 'Am I an American citizen?' and I says 'Shure' and he says 'Come wid me. His Honor needs you'— and here I am." The policeman shook his head in puzzlement.

"His Honor wants to know how deep is the Schuylkill River. If you are an American citizen, you should know such things." Grandpa's gaze went from the officer to the judge.

"Man—be ye daft? And why should I be knowin' how deep the Schuylkill is? 'Tis nonsense yer talking'. I'm not a fisherman or a barge captain . . . I'm a policeman."

"And I'm a tailor," added Grandpa.

"Yer Honor, I don't understand. How deep is the Schuylkill? Would Yer Honor be knowin'?"

"Hrumph . . . of course, of course; you're very right, officer . . . this is all nonsense. You can go now. We have business to attend to, and we don't have all day. I'm sure that Mister Fishman doesn't want to waste any more time."

Still shaking his head at the foibles of people one meets in courthouses, the policeman exited.

"Your Honor wouldn't like to hear the Gettysburg Address?" asked Grandpa, still anxious to please.

"I think it's safe to assume that you know the contents of that document, sir. Will you raise your right hand?" And without further ado, the Judge swore Grandpa into the great fraternity of equality and democracy without any deeper interrogation into the geographic aspects of the Schuylkill.

# 6 Grandma Pays a Visit

My mother's mother was a most wonderful woman with a devotion to God so intense that it probably kept Him constantly on His toes as He tried to live up to her expectations. It must have made Him nervous lest He slip up on protocol, because Grandma was the authority to end all authorities.

My mother is both observant and devout, but she could never live up to Grandma's standards. There wasn't a rule that Grandam couldn't quote regarding *kashrut* and the dietary laws. She drew inspiration from the Talmud, from the Torah, from the Midrash and the Chumish, from Abraham, Isaac and Jacob, from Moses . . . and every now and then, I had the sneaking suspicion that she invented a few restrictions herself.

For most of her dictums, she could quote authority, but when she was stuck for official confirmation, she always could turn to that stock answer that brooked no argument, *"me tur nit,"* which roughly translated meant that the activity in question was out-of-the-question. These magic words were said in a tone that indicated that the consequences of transgression were too horrible to put into words. When Grandma uttered this phrase, we always backed down from dissension and surrendered out of a great respect for what we were sure was a mystic person-to-person line with Heaven or out of the firm conviction that Grandma's martinet disposition could not be challenged.

Grandma was also hooked on certain food fads. She was as sure of the health powers of honey as my mother was of the attributes of chicken soup, and whenever she visited us, we knew that we would be treated to huge quantities of *lecheh* (honey cake).

Now, honey cake is a golden brown treat to the eyes of an epicure; but as far as the taste is concerned, it's like olives, you either like it or you don't. Unfortunately, I belonged to the latter group, the non-likers of *lecheh*. I just didn't care for this nectar which to Grandma wasn't food for the Gods; it was food from God to me. And if I didn't consume every gargantuan morsel, I was guilty not only of lack of taste but of heresy. I had also slipped up in the respect-for-my-elders department. With all of these indictments hovering over my head, it behooved me to try to ingest at least some of the delicacy that was constantly being jammed into my hand.

"Here, *mein kind*," Grandma would say, as she served me a piece that was at least six inches square and weighed half a pound. "Ess, ess, don't be ashamed."

As I choked on the first sicky-sweet bite, she would turn with a pleased reprimand, "Don't eat so fast. There is plenty more."

Her reassurance was enough to drive me to tears, and

as soon as she removed her penetrating gaze, the cake would find its way into my pockets. It made remarkably peculiar fertilizer for my mother's potted rubber plants; it became a mainstay in the diet of our tomcat, affecting him like catnip. The children in the neighborhood loved the stuff although they were too easily satiated to take it all off my hands; I found that even the starving sparrows refused it after awhile and left the crumbs for me to sweep up before Grandma noticed.

She was a tiny lady, but there was something in her demeanor that robbed me of any ideas concerning my personal liberties. I just had to let her live with the delusion that I was a honey-cake lover. Everyone in the family reacted to Grandma in just the same way I did, from father on down. Honoring her every wish no matter how inconvenient it might be.

For instance, Grandma loved to *doven,* and her prayers were long, passionate and tearful. For a tiny person she had remarkable resonance, and as she warmed up, the wailing wall of Jerusalem took shape in our living room. And at that wall, she stood, with much moaning and pounding of the chest.

She was an early riser, and we were often awakened by the sound of her morning devotions. Her obligatos were so startling that invariably some sleep-drenched not-so-early bird would stagger down to inquire foggily, "Who's getting murdered?" Mama, however, could never bring herself to ask Grandma to modulate her tones no matter what happened to our sleeping habits.

But as spring approached and Grandma moved toward the open windows, we wondered what effect her early-morning incantations were having on the neighbors. We tried to convince ourselves that they would respect her religious fervor, and we were entirely unprepared for the conversation that Mama overhead one day between Mrs. Shea and Mrs. Quinn.

"And I always thought she was such a nice woman," said Mrs. Shea.

"I did, too, and I wouldn't have believed it if I hadn't heard it with my own ears," said Mrs. Quinn.

"Imagine a daughter beating her own mother . . . and she such a tiny thing."

"That poor old lady! I heard her again today. Such a-pounding and a-moaning. I was about to call the police, I was."

That was enough for Mama. She still didn't have the courage to speak to Grandma, so she solved her problem in another way. Every morning she arose at dawn, dressed, and went out on the porch and sat in a rocker in full view of the neighborhood and rocked away until Grandma's last fervent syllable had echoed into silence. Then, tired but triumphant, Mother would return to the kitchen to make breakfast for her brood.

# 7  My Bobbe Mary*

My paternal grandmother's name was Mary, and when I mention that fact, there are those among my friends who raise an inquiring eyebrow, because not too many Jewish people of the older generation had names taken from the New Testament. Molly, Maite, Miriam: these were all common . . . but seldom a Mary. Today, and even in my middle-aged generation, one finds the names of self-conscious Americanization: the Irvings, the Shirleys, the Lindas, the Donnas—even the Noels—but in Grandma's time, there were still Sams and Sauls and Isaacs.

The last name was even more questionable for a Jew—Newell *noch*—not Goldstein or Baruch or Cohen but Newell! A name taken from English nobility say the snootier echelons of our family while the more flippant and more realistic members of the clan insist that our name was originally something unpronounceably Slavic and that some Ellis Island clerk, acting as a self-appointed

* Reprinted from *Jewish Digest*

godfather, christened Grandpa with his own Anglo-Saxon name. This was often the custom of the day, and "christened" was certainly the right word. How much more *goyish* could they have been? Mary and Peter Newell? Maite and Peyse had indeed been Anglicized.

Grandpa knew little about his background: he had been a *chapuncheka*, a small Jewish boy, who had been kidnapped to serve as a substitute for some other child being pressed into service in the Russian army. His memories were all hazy. Befriended as a boy by an Englishman, he spoke Yiddish with an overlay of a British accent. This Englishman is also a matter of some controversy in family circles. The *nouveau riche* again imply grand things in the manorial tradition of a Lord Bountiful: the less impressionable and less-out-to-make-an-impression group speculate that Grandpa's benefactor may have been a wandering peddler. Whatever the case, Grandpa was on his own at a very early age.

Somewhere, somehow, in a remote section of Russian Poland, he met and married Grandma. She was the oldest child of a widowed father, and had acquired a great deal of experience taking care of younger children and managing a small farm. She married Grandpa and kept right on managing.

Grandpa had died before I was born, but from what I can gather, he was a sweet, smiling, ineffectual man: Grandma ruled the roost that eventually contained nine little chickens. Only the younger three were born in America; the rest of the brood were hatched in some remote corner of Poland.

How Grandpa and Grandma managed to get them all across the Atlantic to America, no one knows. Their destination was a small town in which they had an uncle who was a *matzos-maker*. Whether his business was too seasonal to employ such large numbers of people or whether he was just unhospitable, he did suggest that they might do better in a neighboring town where there were mills seeking help. They had little choice but to do as he suggested, and so they arrived in a dingy little place where Jews were still a novelty. Grandma immediately went house-hunting and found a third-floor, cold-water flat facing the Erie Canal. The landlord asked the traditional question, "Any children?"

"No," she replied flatly.

Imagine the flabbergasted dismay of the man when he saw the scraggly horse and dilapidated wagon, loaded with an array of shabby furniture, rolled-up mattresses, feather bedding and six boisterous young persons perched aloft.

"I thought you said you had no children," he protested.

"You call those *momserim* children?" she screamed. "They're big enough to support me."

He was either awed by her nerve or frightened by her loud voice because he let her stay. And she meant every word; the children were dispatched immediately to jobs in the dingy, airless, poorly-lighted firetraps they called mills. These were her children's schools and playgrounds.

Grandma and Grandpa found themselves jobs, too; they worked in a slaughterhouse "flicking" chickens—pulling out the pinfeathers that Jewish law forbids removing with scalding water. It was dirty, tiring, smelly work; but Grandma dived in with the passion of one who must have money. More babies came along, but her feverish drive never stopped.

Through an act of God, she became friends with the landlord's wife; not chitchat friends, because unlike other women she never had time for gossip or idle talk. This association began one night when Grandma was roused from her bed by the landlord, frantic with anxiety. His wife was in labor, screaming with pain and panic, and he could not get a doctor. Midwifery came as naturally to Grandma as did taking over; she helped out efficiently and continued to help out during the woman's difficult first days with the new baby.

The woman was not unappreciative. That year she sold Grandma a store which she herself had inherited, a small candy store on the banks of the canal, and in a day of few credit arrangements, Grandma could "pay her out."

Over the store went the sign, "M. Newell and Company," and Grandma became a business woman. She had no trouble with the canalers. Her curt manner was a match for their blustering Irish boisterousness. She insisted on speaking English at all times and her command of the language soon became excellent. She did not need the security of a ghetto neighborhood—in fact, she despised such a need—and desired only to shoulder her way into this new American society of equality and opportunity.

Business ability was in her genes; she bartered and figured with lightning speed, conversed with customers, issued orders, hustled people in and out without a break in the tempo of her financial stride. The shelves were filled with a miscellany of articles: staple groceries, yard goods, notions, high-button shoes, straw hats, and big jars of penny candy. An old roll-top desk, bulging with bills and ledgers, presided over one corner while a black pot-bellied stove with isinglass eyes watched every day as the stream of customers increased. Polish mill hands, Irish canalers, Jewish *landsleit*, they were the constant parade marching to the accompaniment of alien tongues.

The older childen continued to work while the younger

ones were pampered by being allowed to attend regular day school. In fact, Grandma had begun to make bigger plans—the baby would go to college. Soon after the store was established, Grandma bought a barn across from the store and embarked in a new business—rags and metals, and by the time I grew up, her junk business was a town legend.

Grandpa busied himself; he made fires in the pot-bellied stoves in the house and in the store and in the barn. In his bumbling fashion, he cooked for the children, and served as housekeeper and sounding board for Grandma's screaming frustrations. This was not the traditional Jewish home where the richness of Torah was mouthed or where Friday night suppers were served on fresh white cloths after the candles were lighted; nor was it a home of over-abundant maternal care and Godly blessing.

Instead, there were big pots of boiled potatoes and eggs; there was squabbling and constant talk of rags and copper prices. Grandma stayed in the shop to issue orders in Polish to her helpers or to sort rags into bins while the children managed for themselves in the confusion of her multiple interests. She had the habit of squirreling particularly valuable finds all over the house, even under her bed, while the chickens and ducks she raised wandered in and out of the kitchen at will and roosted wherever they pleased. Periodically, a *ponyee,* a Polish woman, would come to straighten up the clutter, but as soon as the work was done, Grandma would again begin to accumulate a disorder of miscellaneous objects.

This passion for collecting extended outside the house, too, as she bought and stock-piled rusty iron and bent copper. Gradually, the huge mound which could mean wealth grew, and she guarded it jealously. On long summer nights, she would sit on her front porch and wait lest some urchin make off with a fragment. In her business, theft was an ever-present factor, and a junkman could be duped into buying any kind of stolen goods, even something stolen from his own inventory. Clients had neither honor nor bills-of-sale for their goods, and a junkman or junklady always ran the risk of being a "fence" for ill-gotten gains. It is a business in which questionable ethics are accepted procedure, but Grandma was equal to any situation. And she had patience; she bought and saved and waited until World War I depleted her hoard and left good hard cash in its place.

Grandma was not a sentimental mother or a sentimental grandmother. When a child married, he ceased to be an economic asset. Two daughters remained in her good graces because they had the sense to marry wealth; her two eldest sons fell from grace for marrying at all. For her, the closeness of Jewish family life did not exist, and when her two sons went into business for themselves, they found her a tough competitor.

I remember my grandma, too, but I know that she never kissed me. My memory is clear of an evening a long, long time ago. My mother and I met Grandma quite by accident as we came out of the kosher butcher shop. They stopped to chat and I occupied myself with inspecting the crates of live chickens piled up outside the market. Restlessly, I shifted from one foot to the other and concentrated on making puddles in the dirty snow that mingled sawdust and feathers.

Mother must have shown me off, her youngest, in pride. I looked up and saw Grandma, in her black hat and black coat. There was no over-effusive friendliness; I don't remember any smiles or any questions. I do remember that she reached into a voluminous black pocketbook, took something out and placed it in my hand. The something was a dime. No kiss, no handshake—a dime! Other people must have the same memory of the elder John D. Rockefeller. I remember, too, the feeling of a great distance between this lady and me.

Some time later, I recall the sadness of my parents at Grandma's death. I was sorry that for me she had never really existed, or perhaps more accurately, as I realize now in moments of dejection, I never existed for her.

My own children are blessed with two grandmas. They snuggle in ample laps and struggle to escape too many caresses. They receive cookies and candy and small precious gifts of toys and buttons and old pots and highheeled shoes—indulgent, useless gifts that children love to hoard. They are showered with all the extravagant endearments that are the language of grandmothers.

*"Mommele, mein Schoen kind, schoen vie der velt . . ."*
This is part of their heritage.

# 8   In the Style of Peyton Place

When Pop's family landed in America, they were welcomed by a *landsman* who escorted them to a flat on the East Side in New York. He sold them mattresses that were well-stocked with bedbugs and wished them luck as he took their money. Grandma stayed a few days and then decided to try her luck elsewhere. She packed whatever belonging were still uninfested and left the bedbugs behind.

It wasn't an easy matter to move, because in addition to their own children, Grandma and Grandpa were also accompanied by her only brother, Hirsch, and a boy named Label who cried because no one had come to meet him at Castle Garden. Somehow or other, they managed to find their way to the little town that was to be their home.

There were a few Jews in town already: the Applebaums, the Chin-Chins, the Kahns, and a tailor with the poetic name of Raphael Allen. Since stores carried no ready-made clothes, he did a thriving business. There was Joseph Pepper, the little crippled grocer with the beautiful wife. "Her parents made her marry him," said the gossips, and they were probably right. In those days, children did as their parents said.

Mr. Kahn ran a general store which grew into one of the town's finest enterprises. He himself served on the Chamber of Commerce and did his utmost to build up the town's image. One lasting memento of Mr. Kahn's presence in our town is the dedication on the city hall, for in a place that is predominantly Catholic and over the years has been ruled by groups of Irish or French or Polish extraction, the inscription on the most important landmark is the work of Rabbi Abba Hillel Silver.

The Chin-Chins and the Applebaums were related and although Mr. C. was very ambitious, Mr. A. wasn't. At least, he did not seek personal grandeur. If he could incite a small revolution, he would be satisfied. With typical Samovar sentimentality, he would bemoan the fate of his beloved Russia (he was German) and spout random phrases from Karl Marx. Since no one in his audience had ever read *Das Kapital*, they were impressed by the quantity of his quotations even if they couldn't check on the quality. To allow Mr. A. time to lecture to the neighborhood idlers, Mrs. A. peddled sheets, pillow cases, and yard goods and considered herself honored to be married to a scholar. His favorite debating crony was an Irish Catholic priest who visited the Applebaum menage almost daily. At least, he did until Grandma mentioned the fact that people were talking. After all, she said, the Applebaums did have two pretty daughters who were to most viewers more interesting than politics.

The priest was not insulted. Instead he commented, "Madam, it seems your people are just like the Irish—practical to the core." With that, he tipped his hat, said "Good-bye" and came no more.

Mr. Chin-Chin was totally unlike his brother-in-law, Mr. Applebaum. He never had time to talk. In addition to working as an apothecary, he was always busy concocting formulas of his own. As his wife screamed that he would blow the roof of the house off, she evicted him from the basement. Grandma, who lived on the third floor, let him work in the attic. It was more convenient there, anyway, and considerably closer to his target. However, for all his wife's mistrust, Mr. Chin-Chin knew his business. His sons, who became chemists and changed their names to something less Chinese, eventually marketed one of his hairdressings for a price that made them all millionaires.

But all kinds of talk keep a small town buzzing and the big buzz of the day concerned the charming daughter of a wealthy undertaker who had become involved with a traveling casket salesman. Since he happened to be both married and Jewish, the populations of both faiths were scandalized. To do him some credit, he did offer to divorce his wife and give the child his name. Being a Catholic, however, she could not marry a divorced man, but she did name the baby after him. The years passed and she went on to become a prominent career woman, and the town, like all towns, eventually turned its attention elsewhere.

Grandma, in the meantime, was not wasting her efforts on gossip. There were too many other things to be done. It bothered her that the Jewish people of the town had to rent a hall for services, and it also bothered the renters who thought the Jews were too noisy. At her instigation, a synagogue corporation was set up and a small two-story frame house on the main street was purchased to be used for purposes of worship. Pop became one of the first presidents and spent a good deal of his time in rounding up seats and fixtures and other necessities.

He heard that St. Rita's Italian Church was remodeling and found that Father Valenti would be happy to donate pew benches if they could be hauled away. Pop did the hauling and then found a cabinet maker to eliminate the carved crosses at the end of each bench and replace them with Stars of David. The man worked long and hard and eventually the task was accomplished. This same gentile man also contracted to build the ark, and as he painted the dedicatory plaque over the top, the names of Grandma and Grandpa, Maitë and Peyse, became Mary and Peter.

As the synagogue started, so it remained. The building grew no larger; the population grew smaller. The benches from St. Rita's still stand in stolid rows facing the same hand-made ark; the curtains Mom made to separate the men from the women wore out and were never replaced although the rods and rings are still there. Only on the high holy days was there light and sound in the little two-story frame house. There was enough money in town to do better—there always was—but the people who cared were long gone.

# 9   A Christmas Story*

Christmas was coming and in our schoolroom we busied ourselves with holiday preparations. Every day I begged bright balls and strings of electric bulbs from my father's store to bring to school. I know that all of this was forbidden to a Jewish child! but tinsel and excitement filled my head, and I pushed all guilty thoughts aside. I sang the Christmas carols with mental reservations and skipped over certain words that I could not sing in conscience. As the others chorused, ". . . Our Lord, Emmanuel," I felt a twinge of self-conscious pride, for that was my brother's name. In Hebrew, it meant "the Lord is with us." How startled my friends and my teacher would be to know that I felt a kinship to the little Lord Jesus . . . He and I were the same kind.

Our Christmas tree filled the room with its fresh pine fragrance that erased all the odors of chalk and sneakers and too many children. We worked hard, and when its branches were completely decorated, we were almost overcome by pride and awe. All the room needed was a final

* Reprinted from *Jewish Heritage*

clean-up before the party. The teacher, in a moment of generosity, acknowledged my supplications and granted me the highest privilege of her realm. I was designated to wash the boards, and Peggy Ann, the girl who usually had the honor, was to be my assistant.

I was too gleeful to let Peggy Ann's displeasure bother me; I was too filled with importance. I ran out to the lavatory to fill the basin. Then balancing the basin carefully, so that I wouldn't spill a drop of water, I returned to where Peggy Ann waited. Silently, we dipped our sponges into the water, wrung them out with housewifely competence, and then began tracing horizontal patterns on the black slate. Concentrating so that there would be no streaks, I worked slowly to prolong the joy. Peggy Ann glanced at me now and then, and I felt a growing elation that I had been allowed to share the spotlight of the teacher's favor with her. Peggy Ann was everything I longed to be: with her brown hair and blue eyes, she was like the flat children who peopled our Reading and Health books—children who were real Americans, who really belonged.

My own black hair and dark eyes made me more like the foreigners in our more exciting but less acceptable geography book. My friend in class were like me, too. They were outsiders: kids who had long, funny Slavic names, or Italians who were as dark as I.

But now—now I dared to hope—I would have a real American friend, one whose parents and grandparents spoke English and nothing else. In the few moments I was rinsing the boards, my daydreaming magically germinated this seed of acquaintance into a "best-friends" attachment.

That dream friendship had become so real that when Peggy Ann leaned toward me, I responded eagerly, ready to share any silliness. Then suddenly, her words came, vehement and distinct, "Christ-killer!"

I was stunned . . . I blocked my ears . . . I did not want to hear.

As the full meaning of her words penetrated, I shrieked, "I am not . . . I am not . . . I never killed anyone, do you hear? I never killed anyone . . ." My voice was shrill and hysterical.

Miss Carleton, the teacher, stood over us. Shaking her head, trying to quiet me, she said something. What it was I don't know.

All I remember was my own anguish and my own sobs and my own voice, as I cried over and over "I never killed anyone . . . tell her . . . tell her . . . tell her . . ."

# 10   First Communion

A little girl can't help being fascinated when a friend dresses up in a lacy white frock, dons a filmy white veil, and takes part in a long procession complete with pomp and spring flowers. The religious significance of the ceremonial escaped me but the pageantry held me enthralled —my friend looked like a bride, one of many little girl brides.

"Ma, when can I make my first communion?"

"What a question! Jewish girls don't make first communions." That took care of that. Something in Mama's voice told me that I had touched upon a topic that was taboo so I asked no more questions.

Veronica, my best friend and next-door neighbor, told me all about the ceremony that was to take place in the Grotto of Our Blessed Lady, and I listened attentively to her every word, as I did to everything she ever told me. Veronica was my ideal, the last word in style and culture and general knowledge. Her blonde hair hung in heavy curls à la Mary Pickford, a very glamorous style indeed compared to my tightly braided straight black locks. She had a wardrobe of crêpe dresses that she wore with wide patent-leather belts hitched tight just below her protruding tummy. Not being sophisticated enough to know that abdominal and dorsal protrusions are not generally considered seductive, I regarded her curves with envy.

In the privacy of Veronica's bedroom, I "oohed" and "aahed" over her white wardrobe—the white pumps, the white stockings, the white crinoline, the white frilly dress —and I was completely gone over the pièce de résistance: the white veil with its small orange-blossom tiara.

"Can I try it on?"

"Sure, why not?"

I was sure there was a why not but I resisted thinking about it because I couldn't resist seeing my straight-banged, dark-haired image adorned in bridal loveliness. As I stared into Veronica's mirror with guilty satisfaction, I was sure that I had never looked more beautiful.

Veronica yawned. She's not the last bit impressed by my appearance, I thought; in fact, I was a bit hurt by her blasé attitude toward my transformation from mundanity. But Veronica was always blasé, I reminded myself, as I soothed my own hurt; it was part of her charm.

"Let's play," she said.

"All right," I said.

We finally settled rather aimlessly on the side porch of my house.

"Wanta play school?" Veronica asked.

"Nah," I responded coolly.

"Hospital?"

"Nah."

"House?"

"Nah."

Silence—long and uninspired.

"Why don't we play First Communion?" This voice was mine, making an effort to sound offhand.

"O.K." Veronica's response lacked enthusiasm and further suggestion.

With that, we decked ourselves out in my mother's old lace curtains, salvaged by sudden inspiration from the rag bag. I found a few dusty wax flowers in a vase on the front hall table and our costumes were complete. The game was hurried for I kept glancing over my shoulder to make sure I was out of the maternal line of vision. But I knelt, following Veronica's lead, bowed my curtained head, clasped my hands as a part of the reverential tableau and expected at any moment to be struck down by the combined wrath of Abraham, Isaac and Jacob. In fact, if Moses had ascended the steps of our porch and shattered the holy tablets of stone over my bowed head, I should have been stunned but not surprised.

"Come on, Miriam." Veronica's voice broke into my reverie of private communion. "This is no fun. Let's play house."

"All right, all right." I answered as I retreated hurriedly from this excursion into forbidden territory. Soon, our veils were draped over the porch railing as make-believe curtains of a make-believe house in a safe non-sectarian make-believe world.

# 11  My Nice Jewish Playmate

⚫○⚫○⚫○⚫○⚫○⚫○⚫○⚫○⚫○⚫○⚫

It disturbs a Jewish child who does not know other Jewish children to meet one of their own who does not quite measure up. For when reality does not conform to a preconceived ideal, there is a danger that the isolated child will make quick generalizations about the whole group from the actions of one individual; from such seeds blossom intolerance.

There I was: Whom did I play with? Who were my peers, my compatriots? Sammy Pawolski and Mary Matusik, Primo Santaranglo, Patrick O'Keefe and Charlie Funicello—a real all-American group of which I was a happy member.

Our day-by-day hours of cameraderie were spent playing leap frog and mumblety-peg, marbles and tag; we lost ourselves in such games as Simon Says and Giant Steps and were enthusiastic novices at baseball. There were more boys than girls in this immediate circle, and that suited me fine.

My mother lamented my not having any nice-Jewish-children to play with—she used the expression so often that I was positive nice was either a prefix to Jewish or that being Jewish guaranteed one's niceness. Thus it was with great satisfaction that Mama found our synagogue fathers had employed a new rabbi who had a wife, and a child about my age.

"Mrs. Weiss told me that they have a little boy about ten, *fegele*," Mama told me.

"I'm almost eleven."

"You'll have someone to play with."

"I have someone to play with."

"I mean someone—someone Jewish."

Mama's implication that this unknown child was superior to my friends rankled. I was annoyed even though I tried not to be, and I felt a dislike growing that conscience and common sense told me were unfair; but still every time the matter came up, I had the same reaction. Who needed him?

Jakie came into my life one sunny summer afternoon— at least it was sunny until he arrived. It was my turn at bat, not really my turn because the boys never gave the girls a turn until they were physically exhausted and mentally worn down by nagging requests. I had waited and whined for hours until they had condescended to let me into the game.

I missed the first ball. Despair. The second was a pop fly and my spirits lifted. At least, I had hit the ball. I squared away for the third when Mama's voice drifted through the air.

"Mashela!" Mama spoke wonderful English, but in the middle of a ball game, she had to use the silly Yiddish pet name.

I didn't answer. The ball game was too important; I was going to hit that third ball.

"Mashela!" Her tone was insistent.

The ball, looming large and white, came at me. I swung hard. I missed.

"Hey, Mash," said the boys making it sound like *mush.* "You're getting worse."

I threw down the bat, angry at the ball, the bat, the boys, my mother and Jakie.

They were all seated at the kitchen table when I got there, Mama and the *rebbesen* having tea and Jakie with a glass of milk. Mama was cutting huge slices of brown honey cake and I didn't like honey cake, either.

"Mashela," Mama said, "I want you to meet Mrs. Weisenfeld and Jakie."

"Hi," I said, begrudging even the salutation.

Mrs. Weisenfeld beamed at me, and Jakie smiled a sickening smile. He was puffy-fat and pasty faced, a new kind of boy to me. I wondered what would happen if I pricked him with a pin; he would probably ooze out on the floor, a puddle of white flab. He definitely did not compare well to my brown scrawny baseball-playing colleagues.

"Show Jakie your games and toys," said Mama. "Go Jakie, with Mashela."

"Come on, Jakie," I said, watching as he pried himself out of his chair. He waddled and his pants stuck in places they didn't belong. Obediently, he followed me to the summer kitchen which had become my private playroom.

I no longer played with dolls but I had a collection which I kept seated in a neat pretty row on the window bench my father had specially constructed. In the middle of the bevy was my pride and joy, a bisque-faced beauty named Rosalinda. She greeted me with her usual brown-eyed, long-lashed stare and smiled a china smile which showed a row of tiny white china teeth. I noted that her lace bonnet was a bit askew and carefully straightened it over her blonde curls.

"Do you want to play checkers, Jakie?" I asked half-heartedly.

"No."

"Jacks?"

"No."

He was picking up my Rosalinda.

"Boys don't play with dolls," I suggested.

"I do."

"Not her," I said, "I'll give you another one." I reached for Betsy, my rag doll.

"I don't want her."

"Please, Jakie."

I grabbed for Rosalinda but he pulled away. As he ran to the other side of the room, he clutched her tight to his overblown shirtfront.

"Give her back to me, Jakie, or I'll tell my mother."

"I'll give her to you," he said vehemently. I stretched out my hands, but he avoided my grasp by walking toward the window. Before I could anticipate his intent, he lifted Rosalinda far over his head and brought her down hard against the bench.

"Here," he said as he handed her over with a satisfied smile.

I looked at my Rosalinda. Her plaster legs were pathetically shattered; her bisque smile was cracked; one eye hung grotesquely closed.

"You're a mean boy—you boob, you fatso." No expletive could be cruel enough. "You're a rat . . . a dirty rat . . . you, you Jew!"

Jakie drew up sharply as the last insult caught his attention.

"Ma, Ma," he started to scream, "she called me a Jew."

Mrs. Weisenfeld came rushing into the room and gathered Jakie's blubbery head to her blubbery bosom.

"There—there—Jakele," she said, "*tattele*, little father, what did she do to you?"

"She called me names."

"Why did she call you names?" said my mother as she caught sight of my Rosalinda sprawled on the window bench.

"For nothing," he said. "She called me a Jew."

"*Oi veh*, my poor boy," moaned Mrs. Weisenfeld.

"That's no name, Jakie," my mother said. "You are a Jew and you should be proud of it." Her tone of judgment sounded as if she were Solomon and Deborah all rolled into one, and some note of maternal dedication to justice came through to Jakie and to me. He stopped crying and I began.

"He broke Rosalinda," I sobbed. "He broke her on purpose."

"My Jakie wouldn't do such a thing."

"He would, he would—he did." My sobs were hard and heavy now, as Mother cradled me to her bosom with her brooch scratching the side of my face.

"Daddy will fix Rosalinda," she said.

"He can't." My sobs became hiccups.

"Then we'll take her to the doll hospital."

This intrigued me and the sobs subsided.

"All right," said Mama, "now be quiet. I want you both to be good and play like nice children. Mrs. Weisenfeld and I are going to finish our tea."

They exited and Jakie and I were alone. He waited fearlessly, his beady little eyes staring out over his fat cheeks.

"Don't you touch me," he said. "I'll call my mother."

"I wouldn't touch you for the world," I said. "I wouldn't dirty my hands on you."

His gaze shifted for a moment as he glanced down the row of dolls speculatively. That was long enough. I kicked him hard—right in his paunchy posterior. It was like kicking a marshmallow—no muscle, no fibre, no resiliency.

He turned, his mouth open.

"If you call your mother, I'll kill you," I said, and I kicked again.

I must have had him bulldozed because he didn't call out. At this point, I should have been satisfied, but I wasn't. He deserved more than a couple of kicks in the pants—I looked around for inspiration. Then I had it.

On one wall of our summer kitchen was a built-in ironing board—one that dropped out whenever the elongated door closeting it was opened.

"Come on, Jakie," I said, smiling as though I had forgiven all, "I am going to give you something."

"What? What?"

"Something nice."

"Candy?"

"Maybe. Here—you just open this door and you can have what's inside." I steered him until he stood directly in front of the door. He opened it eagerly and the long stab of hard wood descended full force and hit him on the skull with a resounding blow.

"Oooh," he groaned.

Our two Mamas rushed in again.

"Now what?" said Mrs. Weisenfeld.

"Nothing," I said, "Jakie opened that door and the ironing board hit him on the head. Didn't it, Jakie?" I was close enough to reach down and give him a surreptitious pinch on the thigh.

"Yeah," he said, rubbing his head. "I opened the door."

"Boys," said his mother. "They're always getting into things. Who told you to open that door?"

I pinched him again, and he was silent.

"Hmph," she said. "Just as I thought—nobody. It serves you right for touching things. You always touch things." Her voice rose so shrill that even I felt a momentary twinge for Jakie. Her hand went back, came down, and hit him with a loud smack across the back of the neck.

"Don't touch things, I tell you. I've told you a hundred times not to touch. Next time you remember—you'll get yourself hurt yet."

Mama stared at me and I stared back at Mama. Her eyes held the flicker of a smile and her mouth curved up at the corners.

"Mrs. Weisenfeld," she said, "Come back to the kitchen. You mustn't get so upset. Children will be children. Come —I'll give you my recipe for honey cake."

# 12   I Become a Scholar

Our synagogue had an educational problem; everybody was for education but nobody wanted to pay for it. The men who could *doven* felt that they could teach their own children, while those who couldn't didn't feel the press of necessity. Those who had children cared; those who didn't have children rebelled—as a result, Hebrew education at best was sketchy.

Every now and then a Hebrew teacher came our way. I use the term teacher loosely because whoever he was wasn't hired for that task *per se*. The rabbi was the Hebrew teacher and the cantor and the *scheiheit*—and if we had owned a mimeograph, he would have been in charge of that, too. For the performance of these multitudinous duties, some fortunate man was paid an infinitesimal salary and given living quarters in the tiny flat that was the second floor of our *shul*. Our holy edifice had once been a two-family bungalow which had been converted into a place of worship by men who all fought for the title of founder.

They argued over everything else, too, at their weekly

noncongenial congregational meetings. Papa often took me with him, and as I inspected the big brass spittoons in the men's section or peeked through the curtains that were strung across to separate the ladies from the gentlemen, the same discussions were repeated over and over. The problems, however, remained. Usually, we had no rabbi, and for some reason the congregation never could seem to comprehend, there were few applicants.

My father didn't have the training to teach us, and my mother who had background wasn't sure of how to go about the job. The result was that my brothers had had long periods of rote instruction and longer periods of no instruction as the transient educators came and went. My mother was dissatisfied and when it came my turn, she decided to find a teacher herself—just for me.

Where she dug him up, I'll never know, but he seemed to have been dead for a long time. His watery blue eyes streamed constant tears which wandered down the eroded wrinkles on his cheeks to get lost in the wilderness of his white brushy beard. In the middle of this beard was an opening for his mouth, and the signposts to this opening were the paths of crumbs that constantly collected. As he put his squat hands on the table near mine, I know I felt no compassion or reverence for his great age—only revulsion. This reaction was strengthened as I noted the bagginess of his shiny trousers and the greasy stains on his vest.

If he had been a pauper, I might have been able to work up a little sympathy; but he wasn't. He was a retired merchant who liked the idea of earning a little something —and who enjoyed my mother's honey cake and my father's discussions on the prices of junk. I tried my best to be respectful, my mother's wrath providing the only motivation needed in that area.

He was to teach me both Yiddish and Hebrew—the first so that I could write letters to my Grandma that she could read easily; the second, so that I could read from the prayer book. He came to the house twice a week, but I never became used to his coming. After a carefree day at school, I would bounce through the kitchen door and always feel the same shock at seeing my pedagogue seated at the table. Freudians would probably interpret my inability to remember our appointments as a subconscious desire to blot him from my life—which was true.

We started with Yiddish lessons first: I learned the alphabet, my name, and a letter to Grandma which read as follows:

Dear Baba,
How are you? I am fine. Papa and Mama and the boys are fine. We hope to hear the same from you.

> Yours truly,
> Your granddaughter,
> *Miriam*

This major accomplishment was the result of rote memorization, so poor Grandma must have received the same letter over and over. We never proceeded to a second letter because I was too busy practicing the first.

At this point, my teacher felt that I was ripe for Hebrew; so we began by the same technique to absorb the same sort of basic materials plus some added prayers. Week after week, I memorized and never understood a syllable I uttered.

"What is this word?" I would say as I pointed to a particular spot in the *siddur*.

"Read the English, read the English," was the impatient answer.

One day a horrible revelation crept into my little mind. He really didn't know the individual words either—he knew them only by rote as he was teaching me. He was just an old parrot training me to be a young one.

Suddenly, spring burst in upon us, and through the open window, I could hear the hum of roller skates and the song of jump-rope rhymes. The kitchen became my cage—a cage for a poor pathetic parrot. I yearned to be free, away from my captor with his wrinkles and stains and crumbs. I knew that all of my friends went for their weekly catechism lessons, but that was different. They had the solace of each other's company. I was alone.

A child's mind is pragmatic—sometimes it is even schemingly evil—and mine must have fallen into that latter category. I had already noted that my teacher was slightly deaf, and my instincts immediately aided me in hatching a scheme for his downfall. At our next session, I began by shouting the lesson as loud as I could.

My mother appeared at the doorway. "Mashela, can't you speak a bit lower?" she said. "You're giving me a headache."

"Sure, Mama," I answered obediently as I dropped my voice to a normal pitch. As she exited, my voice dropped lower and lower.

"Speak up," snapped my ancient pedagogue. As my voice swelled with Caruso-like bombast, my teacher nodded agreeably.

My scowling mother appeared at the door again. "Mashela," she said.

"O.K., Mom," I said. The voice dropped to normal, and with her departure, decreased to a whisper.

"Speak up—speak up." Again the pedagogical directive, and again I bellowed forth my lesson.

Mama reappeared in the doorway. This time she said nothing, but I was happy to see she was annoyed. Later, I could hear her discussing the situation with Papa. They spoke freely in Yiddish since they were sure I did not comprehend. They didn't realize what a glib eavesdropper they had on their hands.

Mama was saying that she was sure the man must be stone deaf, because only a post couldn't hear me, the way I recited. Papa agreed that perhaps she could find another tutor. The old man, however, didn't wait to be dismissed. Suddenly, to her surprise and mine, he resigned. He complained that I would not cooperate, that I would not even speak up when I was told. With that, he drank his final glass of tea, ate his final piece of cake and departed.

Years passed and I was left without much facility in the holy tongue—all that I learned was what Mama could teach me, and what I could garner from my own reading (in English). The letter for Grandma that I had mastered was soon forgotten along with a multitude of other accumulated data.

But at the time, I had no regrets. I was a child with a pair of roller skates—and it was spring!

# 13  We Go Up the Ladder

My father was brought up in the junk business owned and operated by my grandma. Today's junkmen possess a vocabulary of delightful euphemisms—their product is "salvage" or "scrap" or " waste"—but in Pop's day, junk was junk.

When he married, he started his own one-man business with empty pockets, a scrawny horse, an antique wagon and a shack he called his shop. His brother, my Uncle Frank, started his own business, also, in an adjoining shack under similar circumstances.

There, on the banks of the Erie Canal, the two brothers eked out a meager living and slowly amassed their pile of pennies. In due time, the pennies became dollars, and they began to buy the small properties that surrounded their places of business. There was no clear title to any of these houses built on the canal banks since the land was state property, so these *ex juris* inhabitants were actually squatters.

Into one of these domiciles, the two brothers brought their respective brides, two girls named Bessie. My mother was called Bessie Eli, and my aunt Bessie Frank. Soon there were babies—a girl and three boys for them, three boys for us. Business prospered and the brothers bought bigger and better homes on the other side of the street.

Babies continued to arrive—this time twins for them and a single for us. I arrived uncompanioned, backward and temporarily deceased. My family have often speculated that this breach of natal etiquette was symbolic of my later warped mental outlook, a point of view which may have some validity.

The doctor had refused to believe I was on my way even though my mother felt she knew better. After all, I was the fourth of her litter. So with typical female obtuseness, she informed the medical gentlemen that he was cordially invited to spend the evening with Pop, to play pinochle and to investigate a brand-new bottle of scotch. His social conscience must have been touched, for he accepted, and while he and Pop whiled away the evening, Mom labored—and suddenly, there I was. Doc took time out from his melds to administer the traditional slap that gave me back my breath and a chance to squall my first "hello."

Mama was delighted. She had been the only girl in a family of nine brothers, and up to this time, the mother of three males; so she found me a welcome change of pace. Mama's family was different from Pop's—they were white-collar workers: tailors, cigar makers, craftsmen who revered the skills and who grabbed at opportunities for learning. They dreamed of their sons becoming doctors and lawyers, and many of Mama's nephews were already started down professional pathways.

Pop's family were different. Money had come from junk, and they saw even more on the way. Pop had learned to read in night school and was a devoted fan of Horatio Alger; and now that his family was growing and his finances were more secure, he began dreaming bigger dreams. He was ready to move up in the world.

He expanded his junk business and then installed gasoline pumps and a tire repair service for the Model T's and the Hupmobiles that were now moving along Saratoga Street. The mechanism of the car fascinated him and my brothers, and at every meal this was all that was discussed. Radio, too, appeared on the scene, and our males puttered for hours with a crystal set that never seemed to work.

The time was ripe for a change. Pop sold the shop and all his little properties to invest in a store (complete with upstairs flat) on the main street. He spent too much for the building, invested even more in renovation, and then went into debt to stock the place full of tires, batteries, radios and fixtures. It was 1927, and he even bought a television set, an apparatus with a big revolving disc that produced odd shadows once in a while. My eldest brother was enrolled in college in a pre-law course, and the plan was that he was to hit it big and then pave the way for those who were to follow. The other boys worked in Pop's store which was doing well; people bought tires and batteries and radios, all on credit, and we were happy.

For me, this neighborhood of stores was a new experience, and I found myself a whole group of exciting friends. Our next-door neighbor, Mr. Miron, a French Canadian gentleman sold yard goods and notions. Mrs. Miron called me Rosie because she said I sounded just like Molly Goldberg's daughter. On the other side was Pott's Restaurant, presided over by a stout Mr. and Mrs. Potts who served fried eggs and baked beans family style to their loyal customers. Below the restaurant was Steenberg's Stationery Store and below that Cohen's Tailor Shop.

Promptly at nine, I began my rounds. First, to Mr. Miron who always had buttons to be sorted and counted.

Then, to Mr. Potts for a plate of non-kosher baked beans and then to Mr. Steenberg's to read the early morning papers. Because he was generously hospitable, I read *the Times, The Tribune, The Daily News, The Daily Mirror* and *The Police Gazette*. Sometimes, this overdose of reading matter would make me dream about electrocutions and gangland wars; but mostly, I only improved my reading rate. Across the street was a speakeasy, which everyone knew was a speakeasy; but I was never allowed across the street to make friends.

My best friend in the whole block was Mrs. Cohen, the tailor's wife. I was nine and she was fifty, but we were completely compatible. Between us were few differences in taste, or for that matter few differences at all! How many wonderful afternoons we spent dressing up in her fancy clothes and high heels and playing house. How many exciting adventures we had in the five-and-ten-cent store! We were fascinated by the sparkling delights of the jewelry counter and deliberated long and seriously over every purchase. The change-counting was my exclusive department because my friend wasn't too sure of her higher mathematics.

Her husband always welcomed me for he knew I helped his wife while away the hours. Their only child had married and moved away, so he seemed to think I filled some kind of void. He courted me with bits of fur and pieces of cloth, but he didn't need to—I would have come to see my friend, anyway.

I remember the day I ran to show her my newest acquisition—my first eyeglasses. She was thoroughly impressed and decided she needed a pair, too.

"Will you go with me?" she asked.

"Sure."

Off we went, hand-in-hand, to the optician's.

"Can you read, Mrs. Cohen?" he asked.

"Of course, doctor," she answered. As he readied his chart, she whispered, "Stay by me, *fegele*."

He pointed to a letter. "Can you read that, Mrs. Cohen?"

"A minute, doctor," she said as she leaned toward me. "What is it, *fegele?*"

"P," I responded.

"P," she echoed.

"Good!" said the optician.

We continued this triple play all the way down the chart. I must have flubbed a few letters because he fitted her with a pair of glasses to a prescription that undoubtedly would have helped me if I were to wear glasses on top of glasses.

"Just for reading," he admonished Mrs. C.

"Wonderful, doctor," she said, leaving his shop happily. No one ever had such a fitting, she told her husband. Her vision was improved one thousand per cent, at least.

She was such a good friend and taught me many things I'll always remember—how to scrape a carp (my mother wouldn't have one in the house), how to scrub a set of stairs (my mother wouldn't let me), and the latest info on how babies were born (my mother was squeamishly avoiding the topic).

Mom was always delighted when I was with Mrs. Cohen and "out of trouble" as she put it. She was even delighted when we went to the movies more than occasionally, although I am sure she never suspected that we detested Shirley Temple and adored Joan Crawford. I personally felt that the Joan Crawford movies were more educational. I was always learning new words—like *illicit,* for example.

# 14 We Move Down the Ladder

Pop's new business prospered, and we were all content. Each evening, we sat downstairs in the store and listened as the strains of *Poor Butterfly* heralded our favorite soap opera, *Myrt and Marge*. We enjoyed the sad little tale thoroughly and then waited to laugh with *Amos and Andy* or *Molly Goldberg*. As it grew late, Pop would go to the cash register and take out enough change for me to buy ice cream cones for ourselves and any visitors who might be present. For ten cents a head, I could get big double-dip cones in the little store around the corner. The man would heap them high and hand them to me in a bouquet that filled both my hands—a bouquet covered with a piece of tissue paper that was mine to lick at a later moment. It seemed as though nothing could happen to spoil our snug little world, but it could and did. It was 1929.

I was young, but I soon comprehended what depression meant—the dusty shelves scantily stocked, the dearth of customers as day followed day, the piles of unpaid bills, the empty cash register—and eventually the large sign that read *Bankruptcy* plastered on our window.

Pop tried to collect his accounts but people had nothing to give him. More and more stores grew vacant on the Main Street, and more businesses closed their doors. The mills, always the town's mainstay, suddenly decided to move South to cut labor costs. Overnight, everything was different.

I learned the meaning of lots of new words in a short time, like mortgage, interest payments, foreclosure. The property we had owned was ours no longer, and we moved back to the same neighborhood from which we had come, to a flat in a three-story house just like the one we had moved out of—only this time, we were not landlords, just tenants. In fact, we were tenants who found it hard to scratch up the rent. The street hadn't changed much— except that the canal was now abandoned and stagnant and the railroad trains ran on limited schedules.

My brother's legal ambitions faded with our finances, and he left home for the gold fields of the fast credit business. It remained for Pop and Mom and the rest of us to try to patch up the pieces.

Pop investigated every possible way of making a living. Finally, he and my brothers bought some old second-hand trucks to lease to the W.P.A. I was his secretary, typing bids in triplicate, trying to help him figure insurance and gasoline costs. We operated on a shoestring, and somehow survived; but no matter how much Pop earned this way, to him it was like charity.

Mom made everything do—she knitted and sewed and tried to make me look presentable. After all, I was a young lady just entering high school. I knew I didn't have much, but I also knew I had a lot more than a lot of people. In a way, I was kind of glad to be back in the old neighborhood. Most of the people I had known were gone, but there were other friends to be made.

Three doors away lived Mrs. Werner, a fascinating little old lady, who looked like a combination of Mother Hubbard and Mother Goose, ran a rooming house. Behind the house, she operated a second enterprise, an apron factory. Her story was romantic enough even for me. As an immigrant servant girl, she had been hired to work for one of the wealthier families in town and had become involved in a romance with the son and heir. Unlike Cinderella, however, she did not live happily ever after. Her husband was an eccentric of sorts and it had become her task to support him as she kept up the pretense that he was a man of means. He could have been had he not made it a practice to expound his political views on large posters which he hung in the windows of every piece of property he owned. The city fathers were offended and raised his taxes. He raised rents and his tenants moved. When he died, he left his little wife with blocks of empty buildings and mounds of tax bills. Only by her own industry did she salvage the house in which she lived with her collie dog and her boarders.

The boarders were fascinating ladies, too; lavender and lace left-overs from another decade. Miss Van Ness, her white curls bobbing, fiddled constantly with an old cameo necklace which hung from a frayed velvet ribbon round her neck. Her pale watery eyes would glisten as she reminisced about the days when her dear daddy was alive. Over and over she told the same stories of her family and her lineage. "I am a direct descendent of President Martin Van Buren," she would say with her head held high and in a tone that indicated I should curtsy and not yawn.

Her chum, Miss Perry, was fragile as the china cups into which she poured our tea. "First, you warm the cup, so," she rinsed the china in boiling water. "Then you pour." Her pale hands would hover over the tea pots with an alchemist's skill and after the ritual was completed, I was handed a cup filled with a pale green liquid. Even with cream and sugar, it was a bitter brew that I learned to tolerate but not to enjoy. My plebian tastes had already been acclimated to plain old Orange Pekoe served dark and laced with three teaspoons of sugar. Miss Perry was such a charming hostess, however, that I could never resist an invitation to tea and usually emerged from her room with a small gift. Sometimes a china figurine or a yellowed children's book, and once, a stereopticon with slides.

Miss Perry and the lady of the house were both deaf, and they spent considerable time in teaching me the mechanics of their collection of hearing aids. Even with an aid, Miss Perry kept separated from the world in which Mrs. Werner bustled freely. She was the kind of person who seldom had time to talk of the past; she was too occupied with baking cookies or pies or blueberry muffins. If she did have a few moments and could find a partner, she immediately ran for a deck of cards for a game of 500 Rummy.

All of my friends played cards with a passion and it was 500 Rummy that taught me all about sweet old ladies. They loved to play and they loved to win. They cheated like sharks and quarreled like cats, and I developed a skill for not playing too well. It was more peaceful. In fact, I grew to prefer checkers to cards; then I had to lose to only one at a time.

They competed for my attentions, too, and although I tried hard not to play favorites, I felt that Mrs. Werner was my special friend. I had the freedom of her house and explored every room; the attic, the library, the den and in so many corners, I would find odd books on criminology and metaphysics and auto-suggestion. It was my pleasure to curl up in a big chair with some ancient tome and get lost from the world.

Mrs. Werner was German, and she loved to tell me all about the old country. This new *fuehrer* promised much —perhaps he would do great things for her beloved land. It was only the early 30's, but this *fuehrer* seemed evil to me. She tried to alleviate my fears by telling me that things were not what the papers said they were. She would even translate the letters from her people back home.

"See, *liebchen*," she would say, "the papers spread only propaganda. There is nothing to worry for." And she would place a tall glass of milk and a big blueberry muffin before me as further reassurance.

I visited her almost every day and even had a key to let myself into the house. Her deafness had affected her sense of smell, and she had a terrible fear of leaving the gas jets on. It had become my job to come in after school and test the burners. There were days I came and left without her even knowing I was there. So it was one afternoon that I stood in the kitchen and listened absently to voices from the other room.

"I'll go now, Clara, your little Jew will be here soon— if you want anything." This voice was very loud—a friend of Mrs. Werner's. Then there was laughter. With that, I let myself out of the back door and out of my friend's life.

# 15   Art for Art's Sake

In the days before I learned that honesty is not always the best policy, I was like many young people with a passion for veracity and often said things which could be construed as undiplomatic or tactless or worse. This is exactly what happened when I offered an opinion regarding an *objet d'art* treasured by my friend Helen. The masterpiece in question was a painting, or rather a calendar chromo, of Christ in which He was potrayed with yellow hair, bright-blue eyes, and vivid red cheecks. The bucolic background was complete with a brilliant blue sky, decorated with roses and cherubs, and the whole daub was finished in shellac and sprinkled with glitter.

Even as an adolescent I had an enthusiasm for art that was encouraged by several members of the family who were professional artists, and I was well-acquainted with the great masterpieces which are so often religious in nature. I had not been asked, however, to Helen's house as an art critic but as one friend waiting for another to get ready for the movies. Since she had to finish cleaning her room, I sat on the edge of the bed while she worked. Finally, she had everything in order, and as a final touch took a small bottle from her dresser and sprinkled droplets of fluid here and there about the room.

"What is that?" I asked.

"Holy water."

"What makes it holy?"

"The priest blesses it."

"Ohh . . ."

I made no comment but was uneasily aware of the fact that I was out of my element. Helen then reached into a drawer and drew out a box.

"Look what my uncle gave me." She lifted the cover to let me see inside. There was the picture.

"Ummm," was the best I could offer.

"What do you think of it?" she queried.

"Well," I answered glibly, "it's no Michaelangelo. In fact, it's pretty frightful and I really don't blame you for hiding it in the drawer."

"Frightful!" Her voice was indignant. "You have your nerve. What do you know?"

I felt exactly like the fellow who has crawled out on a limb and blissfully sawed off his own support. At this point, there was no retreat from my own stupidity, so I kept talking.

"Well," I went on, "I know that it is a bad painting. And I know that Christ never looked like that—that monstrosity." The last words slipped out before I could stop them.

"How would *you* know what He looked like?"

"I don't and neither do you. The only artists in those days were Roman and they certainly weren't going to waste their time on any Jew—"

"And why not, miss?" I wasn't aware that Helen's mother had come to the door and was listening to our discussion.

"Every religious Jew has a fear of graven images—they are always afraid that someone will worship a statue or a painting. But aside from that, it's pretty commonly known that there is no authentic picture of Christ—only a letter written by some Roman official that gives a fair description of Him—and He didn't look like that!" Everything I had ever read on the subject seemed to come back to me, and I plunged on, not knowing enough to stop.

"I think that you had better go," said Helen's mother. "This is sacrilege, and I won't tolerate such talk in my house."

I walked home slowly and berated myself for my big mouth. No Helen; no movie; no anything. I had spoken in pride, pride in my superior knowledge, and all I had left now was that pride, and it was a very cool companion. At that moment, I would have preferred being with Helen despite her plebian artistic tastes.

I didn't mention the incident to my mother because I had been cautioned many times to avoid discussions of religious matters, and I was sure that she wouldn't be pleased by my artistic iconoclasm. Several lonely days passed, and I was quite ready to eat all of my words, even though I wasn't too sure of how to go about it, when the doorbell rang. It was Helen's mother.

"May I see you, Miriam?" she asked.

"Of course, come in."

Mother must have heard the bell, too, for she bustled into the room. With a mother in each doorway, there was no escape.

"Mrs. Mueller," said Mama, "it's so good to see you. Would you like some tea?"

"No," said Helen's mother, "I can only stay for a moment, but I wanted to tell you about your daughter."

Now I'm in for it, I thought. Mom won't ever let me forget this *faux pas*—not ever—I steeled myself for a long chewing out.

"You see, the other day I was very disturbed by something that Miriam said—about there not being any real picture of Christ and all——"

"She said what?" My mother's mouth began to set in an unfriendly line, and her eyes, speaking many unpleasant volumes, stared in my direction.

"So I went to the big reference library downtown, and I asked them about it, and they told me that everything she said was the truth; and I've came over to apologize. She wasn't being sacreligious." Mrs. Mueller told the whole story as I sat squirming.

"No, she wasn't sacreligous," said my mother slowly, "but she was putting in her two cents where they didn't belong. Fools rush in, you know——"

"Well, the truth is worth knowing," answered Mrs. Mueller, "and I am sorry. Come and see us, Miriam."

As I closed the door behind her, I braced myself for what my mother would have to say, and I knew the lecture was going to be said of some length.

"Ah, my scholar, my picker-up-of-little-known facts; when will you learn that a little learning can be a dangerous thing? So, you taught a lesson and hurt a friend? You are an intellectual boob. Your friend shared with you something she thought was precious, something she loved —and you, you became an art critic."

"Ma, I'm sorry, but what can I do?"

"You can do what that woman did. You can go and tell them that you are sorry, and the next time you can keep your big mouth shut."

"You want me to be a hypocrite?"

"No, just thoughtful. To other people, some of our possessions are odd, different. Perhaps to someone else, that picture of Grandpa with his beard is funny; to me, he is beautiful. Perhaps my candelabra is not artistic, but once they were my mother's and now it is mine and I love it. And you, my daughter, are no Venus de Milo, but I love you and I would take offense if someone said that you were less than perfect."

At last I understood the proddings of my heart and conscience, the message which someone older and wiser had to put into words for me to comprehend.

# 16  High School Days

Far back in my youth at Neanderthal High, going steady didn't begin when one had taken two steps from the cradle; and having a male constantly in tow wasn't a fashionable must. Thus, I accepted my datelessness stoically, wistfully listening as my prettier chums recounted description of the De Molay dances and the Tibbitt's Cadet Balls. Perhaps I wondered why I wasn't asked to these functions, but I don't remember even wondering.

I began to have some suspicion as to why I wasn't asked out more often as my cousin became enamored with one of our classmates and he with her. For the first time, I heard the whispers of how *his* Protestant father and *her* Jewish mother objected. All the parents involved tried hard to break up the little romance while we youngsters cheered on the "star-crossed" pair and reveled in their Romeo and Juliet situation. Nothing ever came of it. Both graduated from high school; both went on to college. He progressed to a big career and to more exciting loves, then married high in the socio-economic register while she remained single and occupied with a career of sorts. Occasionally, I would meet one or the other, and there would always be the same questions. "How's Sharon? Do you ever see her?" "How's Bob? Ever hear anything about him?" Things might have been different, but evidently weren't meant to be.

I often thought of what I might do in a similar situation. Would I renounce my heritage for love? Or would I cast aside love for tradition? How would I compromise? Somehow I always seemed to come up with the same answer: if I were to change, I wouldn't be me; and consequently, the love I felt would be different, offered by someone different. The reverse would also be true, and I felt there must be great disappointment in falling in love with one person only to find yourself living with someone else. I grew convinced that there could be no compromise.

Happily, I wasn't confronted with any such decision. Friendships were offered, but never love. Being an agreeable sort of grind, I was worth cultivating to anyone eager to accept partially-correct homework or reasonably inaccurate information. I wiggled my way into a reportership on the school newspaper, wangled myself places on lesser committees and knew I wasn't sufficiently aggressive to get further. I avoided discussions of religion and background and moved quietly through my own small valley of acceptance.

There were very few Jewish girls in my high school class. Two were my cousins who felt I was a bit gauche in the way I occasionally slipped into a Jewish expression. I knew that they were embarrassed for me, and I delighted in making deliberate flubs. And then there was Fegele Brownstein, who was too Jewish for me. A little plump, a little frumpish, a little old-ladyship—she was a real *yente*. Every word she spoke reverberated with the sing-song intonations of middle Europe, and I, in my turn, cringed.

Our little quartet would probably have provided an interesting sociogram for any student interested in intraracial intolerance.

I felt that my gentile contemporaries accepted me, or at least, didn't reject me. Only one of our group, Sammy Schaefer, seemed to hate me for reasons I could not fathom. He took pleasure in badgering me whenever the occasion arose. Yet strangely enough, he knew more about Jews than any of the others.

He sat directly behind me in French class and once in a while, I could catch parts of his whispered conversation with his neighbor—words like "kike" and "sheeney"— words the others never used around me. Each day I grew angrier but said nothing. As the end of the year approached, we began to make plans for our French Club picnic.

"We could all bring something," suggested Miss Chevalier.

"Sure," said Sammy, "I'll bring a ham sandwich for my friend here." He clapped me hard on the shoulder and I reddened.

"What are you blushing for?" he went on. "Haven't you ever eaten ham?"

"No," I yelled, "I never have and I never will unless I decide to take a bite out of you."

Now it was his turn to redden as the class hooted and howled. My victory turned to defeat, however, washed away in a flood of embarrassed tears.

"I can't understand it," my mother said later when I told her the story. "I've known the Shaefers since I came here. They are nice people."

"They may be nice people—but they have a wicked son," I countered.

"Papa," said Mama. "You know the Shaefers—should we speak to them about their boy?"

Pop shook his head.

"It wouldn't do any good. This is what happens sometimes."

"What happens, Pop?" I asked.

"Mr. Shaefer was born a Jew and when he married a gentile girl, he converted. Sammy is their only boy, and he was raised a gentile."

"But, Pop, why should he hate me?"

"Because you're like the half of himself that he hates."

I wondered afterward how this could be and then I thought of how Fegele Brownstein embarrassed me and how I embarrassed my cousins and I began to understand. Perhaps it was harder for Sammy than it was for any of us.

# 17 My First Employers

My first employer owned a loft-style dress shop, the type of place to which women came from miles around for "bargains." These shoppers were under the impression that he was running an outlet for items he manufactured himself, and he did nothing to correct this faulty notion. Originally, he had come to our town to manufacture dresses and had set up shop in this self-same location; but business in cotton was rotten, and he had dresses piled up that no one wanted. The only ladies who came to his door were those looking for a manufacturing outlet which was located up the street and which had a similar corporate name. This other firm made high-style merchandise while his was a house dress line. As bankruptcy stared him in the face, one pert lady after another stuck her head through the door querying, "Is this the outlet where they have seconds on sale?"

On one occasion as he was just about to answer in the negative, the angel of inspiration whispered a little something in his ear, and he invited the lady in. At least, he thought, he might get rid of the stock on hand. She bought dresses . . . and the next lady bought dresses . . . and so did the next and the next. Then the angel told him it was time to restock and he did, eventually moving all of the machinery out to make room for his new enterprise. From that day on the only "Manufacturing" done on the premises was in the minds of his ever-increasing flow of customers.

I was fresh out of college with a teacher's license, no prospects, and a downcast heart. I wasn't exactly the type my employer was seeking, but his son pushed the issue with, "Pop, the kid needs a job." In a day of maximum hours and minimum wages, I reported in at 9 A.M. and left every day at 9 P.M. approximately (which meant later), and my pay amounted to fourteen dollars and ninety-six cents. The first week I worked in the place, I bought a cashmere sweater and had to borrow four dollars from the brother to pay for it.

As a salesgirl, I learned dirty jokes I had never heard before; town gossip that walked in with every customer; information about mark-ups, mark-downs, and discounts for employees. I met society matrons whose body odor was as heavy as their scent, respectable citizens who were prone to shoplift, jockeys who always shopped with their tall wives, and politicians who shopped with their secretaries. I saw the kind of money I had never known existed for many of our clientele were of high-echelon financial status.

All of these people my employer took as they came. He refused to advertise, to cash personal checks, to open charge accounts—and he did well. His overwhelming passion was work, and his drive and energy were boundless; but occasionally, he would take time out to tell me about his rise in the business world and would always start from the time he left Roumania to come to America.

"I was seventeen," he would say, "and I couldn't speak

a word of English so someone got me a job sweeping out a tailor shop. The tailor paid me three dollars for two weeks and I slept in the back room."

"How long did you do that?"

"A year—maybe two—I lost track. But every night after work, I would walk the streets of New York to see if there weren't other ways to make a living. By this time, I could speak some English."

"Did you find another job?"

"Not really—I went in business for myself. I bought an old pushcart and a supply of greeting cards; and after I finished a day of sweeping, I would push my cart uptown and stand where the theatre crowds would pass. Little by little, I made more money and bought fancier cards."

"Did you do that for long?"

"Longer than I thought I would. There was one place under the El I liked because it was busy and sheltered so I didn't get wet on rainy nights. The only trouble was the policeman used to chase me all the time until I decided to do something——"

"What could you do?"

"I decided to rent the spot. I went to the City Hall, and they told me it belonged to the subway company. Then I went to the subway company. The girls in the office laughed when I tried to explain what I wanted but they thought it would be a good joke to send a "green horn" in to see the big boss. The boss listened and told me he couldn't rent the spot because they were going to rip down the El any day and build a new subway station."

"So what did you do?"

"I asked if I could stay until they built and he said he couldn't see why not, since it would only be for a few weeks."

"How long was it?" I was excited by the brashness of

this young man doing business with the transit company; I could imagine him, hat in hand, trying to make himself understood.

"Over two years. By that time, I had enough to buy a new buggy and a horse and a supply of ladies' wear to peddle."

"Did you stay in New York?"

"No, I started West and finally wound up in Texas. It was beautiful in Texas! I even met a fellow who ran a dry goods store who offered me a partnership." He would pause for effect. "Did you ever hear of Neiman-Marcus?"

I would nod, eyes wide, and he would shake his head. "The same fellow who had the dry goods store. I could have been a millionaire if it weren't for her. She didn't like Texas." We both knew who he meant by "her" because if he took too much time story-telling and I took too much time story-listening, we would both hear that voice from the fitting room, "Mr. S.—you're wanted."

Mrs. S., otherwise known as Mama, was my other employer and although eventually I came to love her dearly, our first meeting frightened me silly. At the time, she was wearing a stout honey-colored cocker spaniel draped over one arm and as she ran her bejeweled fingers through the silken ears, she appraised me frigidly. The cocker didn't look any too friendly, either, and as my eyes went from her much-curled hair to that of her canine companion, my mind set up a silly relationship, and I half expected Mrs. S. to "woof" and the dog to echo "charmed, my dear."

It was the first time I had ever been interviewed by a cocker spaniel, and I came away feeling intellectually and socially inferior. Dogs may be woman's best friend but this cocker had served me notice that she wouldn't even have me as a passing acquaintance. She definitely did not see in me any virtue that would even make fraternizing possible.

Mama gave me a big spiel about her Sally, formally known as Ch. Salomé of Holly Downs, American Kennel Association registered, award winner, best of show, and best of breed in many events. She had been purchased as a pet for Mama's younger son who was away in service, and Mama worried constantly about how much he missed the dog and about how much the dog missed him.

But a job is a job is a job and if I tried hard, I might even get Sally to love me. It seemed like weeks before she even made a minor adjustment but finally she did condescend to sit by me and let me rub her ears.

"Salomé, you're pretty," I told her one day, "If you were only a little more like a dog, I could love you." That was the day I had taken her for a haircut, a manicure and a pedicure and had spent more on the whole works than I had ever spent making myself beautiful. I admit that I was jealous.

Mother S. came in, tears streaming down her face. Her nose was wrinkled so that her resemblance to a cocker spaniel had faded into a pekinesy look. Her cheeks sagged and the tears eroded naked pathways in the rouge and powder terrain.

"What's the matter? Has someone been hurt?" I asked.

"Oh, no, nothing like that. I've just been thinking. Salomé is eight years old today and by the time Teddy gets back, she'll probably be gone and he loves her so." I knew sentiment was overwhelming her because she rarely called her son "Teddy."

"Well, he'll get another dog." Somehow this did not seem to me one of the greater tragedies of war. Evidently, however, I had said the wrong thing because now the streams of tears became flooded rivers, and she blubbered as though she was going under in the torrent.

"Now, now——" I consoled her.

"Oh, what can I do? What can I do?"

I was soon to learn that when a hard-headed business woman becomes overburdened with sentiment, there is nothing she won't do, and her emotions bode no good for the hired help—namely, me.

That evening at ten, Mrs. S. called me.

"Can you come up, my dear?" Her tones were buttery. "I'm lonely."

"I guess so." I was reluctant, having had visions of a warm bath and a cozy bed to ease my weary bones and tired corpuscles.

"Get a cab. I need you." Her tones were mysterious as she hung up.

I dressed as quickly as I could and called a cab to take me to her lovely suburban home. The neighborhood was expensive, the surroundings impressive.

"Come in, my dear." She had the door open only as wide as was necessary for me to squeeze through.

"What's the matter, Mrs. S. Are you ill?"

"Well, no, dear; although I am in a bit of trouble. You remember our conversation this afternoon? Well, I did decide to do something. My neighbor has a fine black cocker, also registered, and he's a male and has fine blood lines and all that sort of thing—and every evening he sniffs around here. I never would let Sally out, but tonight I brought him in and I shut them in the cellar."

"Why, that's kidnapping—I mean dognapping."

"Well, I told you I was desperate. Sally has to become a mother so Teddy will have a dog to come home to. That's what every American boy is fighting for—his own home and his own dog and I had to get Sally the right father for her child—a dog I knew that came from the right environment—"

"You're kidding." I shook my head and hoped I'd wake up. I felt as though I were having a nightmare from eating too many dog biscuits for supper.

"Oh, no, I'm very serious and I need your help."

"How do I fit in?"

"Well, my neighbor has been calling that dog for hours now. I want you to return him, the dog, saying you found him downtown. They'll believe you—his owner's name is right on his collar. They'll probably give you a reward." She acted like an old hand at felony.

"Me? I'm not a very good liar."

"Yes, but you have a very good job." There was no doubt about it—she was threatening me.

"Why can't we just tell your neighbor the truth?"

"Because he'd want a pup, and I want them all for Teddy." There was no arguing with either her business or her maternal instincts, so putting the male in question on a leash, I escorted him home.

The owner didn't spot me coming out of her house, because Mrs. S. took precautions and doused all the lights so that I almost broke my neck before I got down the steps and found the pathway. Like a true-blue good Samaritan, I refused the five-dollar reward the dog's grateful owner offered me and backed away hoping my employer and I would both be sane in the morning. Afterward, I learned a few things concerning the parliamentary procedure involved in studding a female canine. The male's owner can ask a fee, or in lieu of fee, demand a pup from the litter. In top-echelon breeding circles, this is costly either in terms of money or a pure-bred pup. Mrs. S's desire to keep all the pups for Teddy was not all pure sentiment: some of her business acumen had crept into the situation, and it amazed me that she was utterly without conscience in helping herself to her neighbor's (or rather his dog's) services.

But the nightmare had only just begun. Sally was on her way to motherhood, with us along with her. We took her for her monthly checkups; that is, I took her. One day, irritated at chauffering the dog from place to place—I pressed down hard on the gas pedal, and was almost immediately halted by a policeman. I heard Mrs. S. say something about an expectant mother and saw the trooper gazing at me quizzically. I wasn't sure whether Mrs. S. had implied that the mother in question was the dog or me.

In the meantime, Mrs. S. had taken in another pet, a stray cat that had arrived at her door one rainy night.

"It's good luck when an animal comes to you," said Mrs. S.

"For whom?" I muttered as I wondered whether destiny had fated me to be a dog and cat sitter.

Francine, however, was a darling. A little tender loving care and she began to grow sleek and lazy and chubby. Actually, she was chubby from the day of her arrival, but she grew chubbier until we realized she was *enciente*. In fact, she was very *enciente* as she proved by presenting Mrs. S. with seven moist little beggers. There was no fuss, no firing of cannon, only a sudden chorus of meows coming from the linen closet.

I wished that Sally would talk things out with Francine but I could see she considered Francine peasant stock—the type that is back in the fields moments later. I could also see her planning a big production with private nurses and an internationally famous medico in attendance. I purposely hid the newspaper the day a feature on Queen Elizabeth's obstetrician appeared; there was no telling to what extremes Sally's aristocratic notions would go.

Finally, the great day, or rather, the great night arrived. Summoned by an S.O.S., I arrived to find Mrs. S. in the basement where Sally was hiding behind some boxes and wouldn't come out. I spent the next three-quarters of an hour watching my employer's well-rounded rear as she knelt trying to coax the terrified dog out of her makeshift sanctuary. As I sat on the basement steps, I felt superfluous and wondered if I should go boil some water and get clean towels. I would have if I had known what to do with them. Finally, however, we did manage to get the shivering dog up into the kitchen, where we wrapped her in blankets and called the vet. It was an hour before he arrived and I took an instant dislike to him. For all his smooth, paw-caressing, bedside manner, he poked Sally dispassionately and callously announced she needed a Caesarean section.

"Hmph," I snorted.

"She's too old to be having pups, she's like a woman of fifty and it's too late for her to be starting this sort of thing now."

I could see Sally didn't like him either.

"Well, you're not operating on Sally," I announced, presumptuously since she wasn't my dog. "You'll kill her."

"Well, at least we'll save the pups." He *was* a cold character.

"And lose Sally? No, thank you." Mrs. S. was overflowing in saline emotion so I took command.

Dr. Burns seemed most irritated as he exited, and his irritation showed in the bill he sent. For what he charged her, he could have birthed all of Noah's Ark. But night

was fast becoming morning and Sally wasn't getting any-
where. Since animal midwifery wasn't my specialty, I con-
sulted the yellow pages and phoned another vet.

This fellow arrived sleepily—a nice young man who
seemed to like dogs, even Sally.

"Well, you're in trouble, old girl. Let's see if we can
fix you up." With that, he gave her a shot of Ergotrate,
patted her on the hind end, and left. He was gone before
we realized we should have kept him.

About a half hour later, I began to learn the facts of
life from close observation. Sally, devoid of any natural
instincts, was no help whatsoever as the little strangers
arrived, all packaged like sausages. No one had ever told
me about these things, so how was I to realize that normal
dogs rip these little sacs off with their teeth? Two of them
were victims of their mother's negligence before Mrs. S.
and I realized what we should do. We rescued three pathetic, wet, little things and turned them over to a disinterested Sally.

Disinterested is putting it mildly; she sniffed at them
and growled. What a mother! Who said foundlings can't
come from parents of quality?

"What do we do now? They'll die." Mrs. S. had again
began to cry, but a few more telephone calls, and she
found a druggist who could be bulldozed into bringing
out bottles, nipples, evaporated milk and other paraphern-
alia. I could hear her on the phone. "My babies are dying!"
She didn't mention that the babies were canine.

She soon had some kind of concoction whipped up and
there I was—back on the basement steps. I tried to force
a few ounces of milk into their reluctant pink mouths, but
they grew colder and colder and looked a lot less promising
than they had an hour before.

Suddenly, I spotted Francine in the box in the corner quietly nursing her brood like a good mother should.

"Aha, my lady, you'll know what to do." I said and dumped the three little orphans in with her. I gambled on the fact that she couldn't count, anyway. She looked at the pups, sniffed, looked up at me as though I were the stork's tardy assistant and took over. Each one was given a brisk bath and a faucet complete with breakfast, lunch, and dinner.

"Francine, you're wonderful." I was overjoyed as I showed Mrs. S. the new nursemaid.

"Oh, I don't know," she was dubious. "I'll call the vet." It was near dawn, but that didn't bother her.

"Doctor, the dog had her pups."

He evidently was not surprised.

"And she won't nurse them."

He evidently again was not surprised.

"Oh no, I don't want to bring them to you to take care of. Is it all right if the cat takes them?

Later, she told me he said that the cat might not be willing.

"Oh, doctor," she tried to make herself clear. "The cat has them. What I want to know is—will the formula be all right?"

I remember giggling hysterically. It may have been from fatigue or just the thought of what I had come to.

The new threesome thrived on the cat's milk augmented by a diet of pablum and chopped baby meat and daily doses of oleum pergamorpham. As they grew glossy and black and fat, I often saw Mrs. S's neighbor look at their tawny mother and then at the three babes with a suspicious eye.

By this time, I was a regular fixture of the household

and spent my time chauffering the two princes and the one princess and the Queen Mother back and forth to the vet's for shots, to the barber for clippings, and sometimes just out for air. Mr. S. had been cajoled into building a huge playpen for them in the kitchen, and during the day, this was kept lined with wall-to-wall newspapers, so that while we were at the store they could take care of the normal functions of life, or they could catch up on the news if they so desired. In the evening, they were allowed out for a romp. As I watched them growing more mature a precautionary notion suddenly occurred to me.

"I really think you should separate them," I said.

"Why, my dear?" Mrs. S. looked surprised.

"Well, they're getting older and everything." I didn't know quite how to explain what I meant.

"Why, they're brothers and sisters——" I could see she was shocked at my implication. These were her dogs and she resented my suspicions concerning their moral rectitude. I explained apologetically that I didn't think they were aware of their sibling relationship, and in their innocence, might—but the look in her eyes told me not to push the matter any further.

However, to make a long story longer, in another six months, both Sally, Senior, and Sally, Junior, were mothers again. One had a litter of seven; the other, five, giving Mrs. S. a grand total of sixteen yipping, yapping cocker spaniels.

The smell of sixteen cocker spaniels is beyond description. It's not the stockyard smell of calves or the earthy smell of a sty but it's comparable. And not only did her home smell like a kennel; it looked like a kennel. In fact, I'm sure that the neighbors were investigating the zoning restrictions relative to businesses in residential areas.

Mr. S. had been very tolerant through it all, but now he began to rebel.

"Mama, we have to do something," he said. "We have to get rid of some of these dogs."

"Of course, Mr. S."

The next day, one went to the milkman and another to the grocer. Each had to answer a long roster of questions concerning environment, heredity, background, *et cetera* and received the thoroughbreds with many misgivings on the donor's part. The letting-out-for adoption procedure continued by fits and starts because occasionally Mrs. S. would retrieve a pup from people she considered "unfit parents," but eventually only three were left.

And eventually, even the war ended and Teddy returned home with a surprise, a brand new bride who was allergic to dogs.

## 18 Russians, Galicianers, Litvaks, *et al*

My mother often made uncomplimentary remarks concerning that portion of Jewry known as Litvaks. She was a Russian, she would tell us, in a tone which indicated that this was tantamount to being a member of royalty. When some minor acquaintance committed an infraction of the established mores—anything ranging from a breach of etiquette to petit larceny—mother could always explain the anti-social action in the light of that individual's national heredity. As I grew older, I learned that the only individuals lower than the lowly Litvaks were the Galicianers, and I also learned that the Russians, the Litvaks, and the Galicianers formed a long-established mutual animosity society.

The joint antipathy of these groups is humorously ironic. Any map of Europe will show that Lithuania, Galicia, and the section of Russian Poland from which all these people stem is an area of less than 150 miles in diameter, so that the feuding factions were actually *landsleit* (neighbors). When Poland suffered its tri-partitite division at the hands of Russia, Austria and Prussia, this Jewish-inhabited area was at the center of the separation; and this political development engendered a triple animosity in people who had no part in the decision. In fact, the Jews, leading a segregated existence, were even more removed from the stream of conflict than their gentile neighbors, but being human, they could not help but mirror the conflict around them. Later generations forgot the cause but sustained the animosity.

Equally odd was the antipathy of this group and the German Jews, strange because the Poles could trace their ancestry to the original settlers of the Rhine Valley, the people who had emigrated to the area in the days of Roman Conquest. There they had lived peacefully until the Crusades, when the Christian fervor flowing toward the Holy Land developed a fanatically anti-Semitic backwash. The Jews tried to escape this tide of hatred by migrating north to Poland where they were welcomed by the controlling princes who needed their skill as traders. In their new home, the Jews remained segregated enough to retain their language, sixteenth-century German. Over the years, the processes of natural evolution added many borrowed or coined words, and their brand of German became Yiddish, a language which middle European Jews spoke fluently and which the German Jew eschewed as an inferior kind of doggerel.

The middle European Jew naturally assumed that all Jews spoke Yiddish and was often surprised to find those who didn't. The Sephardic Jew of Spain or Portugal spoke Ladino, which was a mixture of Latin and Hebrew. Since remnants of this group had migrated to Greece and Turkey during the Inquisition, they never had contact with the German or Polish groups. The modern Israeli

Jews have revitalized Hebrew, and many of them regard Yiddish as a foreign phenomenon.

Such family conditions are common; much has been chronicled regarding the differences between the "shanty-Irish" and the "lace-curtain Irish," the Ukrainian and the Russian, the Italian and the Sicilian. In all cases, tempers have run hot over varied claims to superiority. It seems that arrogant intolerance runs in a man's blood stream, and like some kind of dormant and toxic virus lies ready to take on violent and infectious proportions at any given opportunity.

With the first immigrant group, the matter of who was what was of extreme importance. The older folk could detect a renegade in their midst simply by his alien speech. A Litvak would say "mutter" for mother, while a Russian would pronounce the same word "mitter." The Galician-er's version was closer to "meater." Such a phonetic varia-tion provided a vital point for conjecture. Few people were like my Aunt Annie, who was blessed with a soul for com-promise. Her antecedents were Litvish, but she had been favored by a union with a Russian.

"All I had to do," she would say, "was remember to call my mother "mutter" and my mother-in-law "mitter." Knowing both her mother and her mother-in-law, I was sure that her life was filled with even more day-to-day con-cessions to very adamant elderly ladies. But she probably considered herself fortunate even at that; many a young-ster had been disinherited from his tenement holdings for daring to marry out of the nationalistic fold.

The third generation removed from Europe was even more confused by these boundary-line distinctions. As my young sister-in-law grew into the age when the young men came a-courting, she found herself plagued by the numerous comments that are made all too freely in a large family. One boy was too tall, another too short, another too rich and another too poor. A non-Jewish suitor was taboo, and any interest in that direction was looked upon with a scandalized eye. The poor girl was growing increasingly tired of it all but she could think of no way to stop the critics.

Still trying to please, however, she arrived home one evening with the tall handsome young man who was eventually to become her husband. After running the gauntlet of introductions, she could hear an audible, *"Feh* —he's a Galicianer."

"Look," she answered with disgusted finality, "He's Jewish, isn't he?" And that settled that.

# *19*  Intermarriage

Intermarriage hit our family hard and with the same impact as fire, flood, incest or leprosy. There was much weeping and wailing, moaning and mourning, cursing and caterwauling—but nothing could turn back the tide of impulse.

It began with Uncle Ted and Aunt Sheila, he of proud old Hebrew stock and she of the finest Gaelic extraction. They had been born on different floors in the same tenement on the same day, had gone to kindergarten together, grade school together, high school together—always inseparable. On the day they graduated from college, they were married by a justice of the peace, much to everyone's dismay.

Grandma ranted and raved and swore to disown them, and Aunt Sheila's mother reacted in much the same manner—so the unhappy couple packed and moved and set up housekeeping in a city far far away.

This was beginning of the end. Soon other uncles and other cousins also took that step away from the fold until events seemed to go full circle. Thirty years later when Aunt Sheila protested that she didn't want to attend a clan wedding because it would be embarrassing—that she would be a gentile among Jews—one family wit remarked, "You don't have to feel that way. At this stage of the game, your kind outnumber our kind."

I didn't really understand the full implications of the situation until it hit my generation—my brother. For years, he had been a Don Juan of sorts, a left-over bachelor with an apartment and ideas of his own. As youngsters, we were very close; but as the years passed, he came home less and less frequently. On one visit, however, he did manage to confess to my mother that he was married, had been married for some time, and was, in fact, the father of a six-month-old baby boy. A shocked silence greeted this brace of announcements, but finally mother spoke.

"Son, what is your wife's name?"

"Carrie—"

"Carrie what?"

"What difference does it make?"

"No difference—I thought I might know her family——" Mama's voice shook and her hands trembled.

"Is she Jewish?" Papa was always more direct.

"Jewish, who knows? How does anybody know whether she's Jewish? How do you know you're a Jew? Can you prove it?"

"Don't give me lawyer arguments. I'm a Jew because my father told me, and his word was good enough for me." Papa's voice was angry.

"Hearsay. No court in the world would admit such evidence."

I stared at my brother, and wondered whether he had lost his mind.

"Papa," said Mama softly, "why ask? She's not Jewish. What about the baby, Simon?"

"Oh, he's Jewish, Ma. We had him circumcised and everything."

Mama smiled sadly.

"That doesn't make him a Jew, my son. Did he have a *briss?* Did you get a *mohel?*"

"*Briss, mohel*—do you think I'm a peasant?"

"It still doesn't matter," said Papa, something like a sob coming through his heavy sigh. "The child belongs to the mother, anyway."

At this point, Simon launched into a long discourse on the history of intermarriage, noting all of the notable precedents from Moses to Disraeli to Bernard Baruch.

"Moses, you're not," said Papa, "and you're no Baruch either—and Disraeli, you can't count. He was a gentile, anyway. You're just my son, I'm sorry to say."

It was a jolt but somehow we survived and even tried to pick up a few pieces.

"Mama," said Simon, "I want you to come and meet my wife and her folks."

"Alone?" said Mama, "without Papa?"

"Go," said Papa. "I don't mind." He returned to his newspaper and tried to retain his composure, but I could see the paper shake and I could hear the impatient tap of his foot on the floor.

"Go, go," he said. "Go."

Reluctantly, Mama consented to spend the day in Simon's world. It was a fifty-mile trek to his home and as Mama told us later, he seemed to be driving at about twenty miles an hour. He stopped at every gas station to check the oil, the gas, the air in the tires, to buy a paper, to get coffee . . .

"Son," she said finally, "don't you want to get home? Is something bothering you?"

"Well, Ma," he said, "it 's like this—Carrie knows I'm Jewish, I told her; but her folks think——" He stopped, not knowing how to explain.

"Her folks think you're a gentile? Oh, Simon, why are you such a fool?"

"Well, that's what they think, so would you mind?" His face grew red.

"Would I mind what?"

"Would you mind not saying you're Jewish?"

"I'll mind, but if it will make your life easier, I'll try to help you."

"Good! Thanks, Ma—you're a good egg."

"A good egg, I am? And a good Jew I'm not supposed to be?" She sighed again, and they drove on, the journey speeded up by his relief.

"Son," Mama added, "you are very lucky."

"Yeah, Mom, why am I so lucky?" He spoke without too much interest—his problem solved, his mind was on other matters.

"Well, I was thinking, son—me, you can hide, it's easy. All I have to do is cooperate and be quiet. That's why you're lucky. What would you do if I were a *colored?*"

For quite some time, Simon did manage to hide us all— Mama, Papa, an assortment of aunts, uncles and cousins, two brothers, and me; but it was I who eventually brought a cloud of suspicion hovering over his head. I became engaged and the customary announcement appeared in the newspaper. My surname could have belonged to any- one of undetermined origin but my groom-to-be's cog- nomen was unmistakably Jewish. Or at least this was the scream of my beloved brother as he came in, brandishing the newspaper as thought it were exhibit A in a murder trial: he the prosecutor, and I the defendant.

"The trouble you caused me," he said. "When my mother-in-law saw this, she wanted to know if you were my sister."

"You didn't have to tell her," I said. "I wouldn't have been hurt."

"How could I not tell her? We have the same name, we're from the same city, and we have the same mother." Papa was dead by this time so the announcement had come from Mama.

"That only sounds like circumstantial evidence," I said.

"Don't try to get funny."

"I'm not trying to get funny—I'm only trying to be pathetic like you."

"Ma," he yelled. "Did you hear what she said?"

"I heard, Simon, I heard. So what did you tell your mother-in-law?" Mama's voice was a mixture of sad amusement and curiosity.

"I had to admit it was my sister. And you can imagine the old lady's shock! My sister marrying a Jew!"

"And did you explain, Simon?" Mama said.

"Yeah, Simon, what did you tell her? That it's the fashion for Jewish girls to marry Jewish boys this year— at least for this Jewish girl."

"Don't be crazy! I told her . . . I told her that you were one of those crazy college kids, the kind who's gone on tolerance and that jazz."

I could just picture his mother-in-law offering him condolences for my transgressions.

"My God!" I said, "you're unbelievable."

Mama said nothing, but after he was gone, she did not

move. The afternoon wore on; it grew dark, but she still sat there. I moved to turn on the lamp near her chair and I could hear her murmuring something softly. *"Ish ka dal—ish ka dash—schme rabo."*

"Ma," I turned the switch to bring the cheering light into the room. I wanted to tell her not to feel that way, not to care, to forget him, but I couldn't. She was fragile and tired as I leaned down to kiss her and the eyes that always brightened so easily with smiles were filled with tears.

"What did I do, Mashela? What did I do? What did I do?"

# 20 My Brother, the *Soldat*

Manny is one of those sweet people who live in a world all their own. They are often confusing to the rest of us pedestrian folk but certainly they make our lives livelier. I am sure, however, that had the German high command received word of his enlistment and realized fully its implications, they would have surrendered earlier.

In 1941, Manny was a licensed electrician with more than a little knowledge of telephone installations. He was the kind of man the Signal Corps could have used; but he volunteered to join the Army Engineers because although he didn't mind fighting, he hated walking. I took all of his fight talk with a grain of salt because I knew that he was deathly afraid of lethal weapons. As he would say, "This fooling around with guns and bayonets could get a guy hurt."

Two weeks in the Engineers convinced him that he had made a mistake, but there was little he could do about it. He didn't even get time to complain before he was on his way to Merrie Olde England accompanied by about three hundred company mates, most of whom hailed from the backwoods of Kentucky.

To Manny, these fellows were a new breed of gentile. As an electrical worker employed by the police and fire departments in an Irish Catholic town, he was used to mild-mannered beer drinkers who invited him to their communion breakfasts, but his new bunkmates were not mild in any respect, particularly not in their drinking habits. Their eating style was new, too.

"Have you ever seen a man butter corn by rolling it in his hands?" he'd say as if the memory were engraved in his mind.

To them, all New Yorkers were Jews and all Jews New Yorkers; and no New York existed outside of the city proper. Luckily, he wasn't too thin-skinned or their opinions of Jews might have caused him to complete his tour of duty in trauma. Then he met the Britishers and their antipathy to Yanks offended him even more.

"Be careful," he would warn, "or we'll cut down our barrage balloons and let this foolish island sink into the sea." Time passed and D-day approached and he was still in England. "Pretty soon I'll be qualified for citizenship," he wrote.

Then we heard the news. Eisenhower's forces had invaded England and we worried. Days passed and no news. Then a V-mail letter.

"Don't worry. I'm fine. In hospital, and will write.

> Love,
> *Manny.*

The things we envisioned were frightful, but still no mail. "He must be wounded," wailed Mama, "and so far from home."

"Mama, he said he was O.K." I tried soothing her. "I'll write to his C.O."

So I wrote but still no news.

"I'll write his chaplain."

Still no news.

Then a letter came. Baby brother had been stung by a wasp family that had nested in his truck, and since he was allergic, he had been hospitalized in Britain. D-day had left him safely and happily cajoling the nurses.

Our relief was short-lived because we received a new letter. Manny had volunteered for a new outfit, a mine-detonating crew. "Don't worry," wrote Brainy. "It's not dangerous if you're careful."

From then on, his letters sounded a bit befuddled as if he were never quite sure of where he was in relation to the rest of the army, because every day we read, "Wonder where Patton is?" "What's Montgomery doing?" Either he was completely lost or just delinquent in paying for his subscription to *The Stars and Stripes.*

At about this time we received a telephone call from a young minister who lived in a neighboring town. He had just arrived home and was coming over to visit because he had promised Manny to look us up.

"We'd love having you," I said, as I wondered why he couldn't deliver his greetings by phone. An hour later, a tall pale uncertain young man on the style of Casper Milquetoast appeared.

"Won't you come in?" I said.

"Oh, yes," he said. "Thank you."

"Won't you sit down?"

"Oh, yes, thank you."

Long silence.

"Manny told me to be sure to see you."

"That's very nice of you. How was he when you left?"

"Fine. Great."

"Was he working hard?"

"Well, not really." Then he began to tell me about what Manny did. He and his aide (the minister had filled this position) worked alone with a little truck filled with tools and explosives. Manny soon told him that they'd never be able to operate with all that junk.

"Operate what?" he had asked.

"Just operate." The first step was to unload the explosives—right into the river—then to requisition a few things.

"You can't visit people empty-handed," Manny told him. A hospital supply depot nearby had canned hams and pineapple juice and chocolate and soap and a requisition was easy to forge.

"No one ever went near our truck marked *Danger: Explosives*," he explained, "so it was easy to operate."

"Operate?" I said.

"Operate." He shrugged, nervously turning his hat in his hand. There was a long silence and I supposed his visit to be at an end. I rose to escort him to the door.

"You know," he continued, "I never did a wrong thing in my life until I met your brother. I never smoked or drank or went with——"

"Girls," I supplied.

He nodded again, and I began to speculate about this timorous confessional. Was this why he hadn't delivered Manny's messages by phone? Did he by any chance think that Manny's sister was as adventurous as Manny? I remembered the picture of me Manny carried, a beach shot with a striking silhouette.

"Well," I said, "now that you're away from him, you can mend your ways."

"But I miss him terribly."

"Yes, we all do." I remained standing so that he finally felt obliged to get up, too.

"I'm sorry you missed my mother," I said. "But I'll tell her about your visit. She'll be very grateful."

"I could come back."

"No, we couldn't put you to all that trouble." I shoved him out the door and slammed it with some finality on him and all his wistful dreams of operating.

When Manny did finally arrive home, he was nervous and jittery and plagued by nightmares that stayed with him even through the day. All he wanted to talk about was Scotland where he had had a furlough far from the war. The brash ridiculous soul we all knew was much subdued. All of his belongings lay heaped in his room until one day I decided to get him to straighten up.

"Come on, I'll help you!" I offered, reaching for a shirt draped over the chair. "This will look better on a hanger."

There was a small clang as a set of dog tags dropped to the floor. I picked them up and idly read the notation. There was his name, rank, serial number followed by a small letter *C* in the bottom corner.

"Doesn't this stand for Catholic?" I asked. "Did someone make a mistake?"

"No mistake." His face was red. "Those are extras." He opened his shirt to show me the pair he still wore.

"Extras, what for?"

"Never mind—they're just extras."

"How did you get them?"

"I just got 'em."

"But why the *C*? You're not Catholic."

"Look, sis," he said with the patience he would use talking to a small child. "You're a teacher, but you're not too smart. I was in the front lines, sometimes even beyond them. I could have been captured any time. Now you know I'm Jewish, and I know I'm Jewish but can you think of any reason the Nazis had to know?"

I shook my head. My silly brother knew a lot more about what he was fighting for than I had ever given him credit.

# 21  Mike Plays Santa Claus*

It was 1944 and the war news was not good. As the Germans massed for one last push, American troops from all over Europe were being rushed into Belgium to protect our hard-won entry at Antwerp. These were the days preceding the Battle of the Bulge.

Mike was stationed with the 995th Signal Corps Brittany and had been writing every day—wonderful letters which would have minimized the war into non-existence had it not been for the fact that I read the papers. "We were the last ones to hit the beaches," he wrote. "We came in just after the WACS. The colonel made us wade ashore from the landing craft because he thought we might make the newsreels. He kept promising a protective umbrella but it never arrived and we could have used it—in that rain." He wrote enthusiastically of the French people who not only understood but even appreciated his high school French and liberally illustrated each letter with charming charcoal sketches of the cobbled streets and villagers in their peasant garb and wooden sabots.

The letters did so much to keep up my morale as I

* Reprinted from *The Mennonite*

122

waited impatiently for the days of separation to end. Since my brothers were overseas, Mom and I were alone in a house crowded with worry. I lived the same life that many millions of other women did; I went to work, came home from work, wrote letters and waited for answers. Time promised little more than the same endless routine.

It was shortly after Thanksgiving that I wandered into Woolworth's and aimlessly perused one counter after another. The store was filled with Christmas things—red and green decorations, strings of colored lights, small artificial trees, tinsel and toys—while a record player serenaded the customers with the Bing Crosby rendition of "White Christmas."

What could I buy for Mike? For the holidays, mailing restrictions were lifted, and I had already sent magazine subscriptions, hand-knitted socks and a sweater, several rolls of film, and a fruitcake. (He received twenty pounds of fruitcake that year from doting relatives who, like me, didn't know he hated the stuff.) But what to send? Attracted by the colorful gimcracks, I stopped at the toy counter. Just for fun, I decided to fill a stocking and send it to Mike. After he'd had his laugh, he could pass it on to one of the children he knew. Every letter contained some mention of the youngsters who hung around American billets and followed the soldiers with cries of "*Avez-vous du chocolat? Avez-vous du* 'chewing gum'?"

I picked up a regulation mailing carton and filled it with some wooden soldiers and a set of jacks, a colored yo-yo, and a wind-up teddy bear who clapped a set of tinny cymbals. I stuffed the corners with small bags of hard candies and covered everything with a big red felt stocking. I bought wrapping paper and string, and in a half hour the whole thing was mailed to Mike with a separate note telling him to watch for a *Chanukah* package from Santa Claus.

A few weeks later, I received Mike's reaction—a million thanks for a silly impulse. He had given the box to Yves, a Frenchman who worked in the camp. The man's wife had been killed in a bombing raid by Allied planes as they attacked the coastal regions prior to the beach landings, and he was left to care for their two small sons, Michel and Yvon. He had no money to buy toys for Christmas. It was all he could do to get food; anything else was a luxury beyond his grasp. Then my idiotic package arrived, and two little French boys had a happy holiday.

Mike wrote unashamedly of how he and Yves had wept. "We must have been a sight. He needed a shave and so did I, but he hugged me and kissed me on the cheek. He was so grateful." Enclosed in the letter was a picture of the two boys for Mike to send to the "Mademoiselle from America who is so generous." I cried, too, as I read the letter and looked into the faces of two small boys caught in the midst of hostilities.

Mike also wrote that the 995th, otherwise known as the "Hoboken Heroes" was planning a Christmas party for about twenty-five of the children in the neighborhood. Actually, most of Mike's outfit were from New York City, and to the gentiles in the outfit, they all sounded like Jews. There was a large percentage who were but also a large percentage who weren't. When Mike tried to explain he came from a town upstate, he invariably met with the same reaction, "But all you Jews are big city boys." He was amazed at the number of boys from all over the country, from all sorts of backgrounds, who had never even met a Jew and who admitted rather freely that he was nothing like what they expected. Since he is a burly, six-footer, they didn't also care to be specific about their expectations.

The arrangements between Jew and non-Jew were genial, however. Christian boys took all of the details on the High Holy Days and the Jewish boys reciprocated at Christmas. One Aryan-looking Jewish boy helped the company priest serve Mass for several Sundays before he built up enough courage to tell the *padre* he had picked the wrong assistant. Conversely, several gentile boys mistakenly found themselves attending a Passover seder and stayed because the food was pretty good.

At any rate, the children's Christmas party was to be held in "Ye Old Frenche Chateau," the name the fellows had given to the bombed-out castle in which they were billeted. They cut down a small tree, and they popped corn to string into decorations. No one bothered to ask the cook where he had requisitioned popcorn from; they were just grateful for his contribution. They also collected *chocolat* from every fellow in the company and practiced singing carols in French to entertain the children. As Mike said, "Our French is always good for a laugh."

But the army had other plans. Three days before Christmas, the 995th was moved North to Antwerp. "It would have been fun to make the kids happy for even one day," Mike wrote, "but things being what they are, making plans is folly."

This time, the 995th was billeted in a kindergarten in the center of Antwerp. There had been no time to evacuate the children from the city and each day they gathered in small crowds to beg for pieces of coal. The soldiers, unloading the coal trucks, would purposely drop shovelsful so that the children could fill their buckets. Antwerp was under buzz bomb attack, and many of the children who came to the doors one day did not reappear the next.

On Christmas Eve, as the men sat listening to the off-key strains of "Silent Night" being played on the school's little old pipe organ, some hummed and some crooned to themselves. In spite of the rain and imminent attack, their spirits rose, and as each man wished his buddy a "Merry Christmas," they did not really worry about whose holiday it was.

For the moment, at least, they shared a common wish for a time when there would be peace on earth and good will for all men.

# 22   Another Christmas Story

Jewish children love Christmas trees, for the same reason Gentile children do—for the gay ornaments, the silver tinsel, the balsam smell, for being the symbol of gay festivity—for Christmas is, after all, a children's holiday, a children's dream-come-true.

Sooner or later, however, Jewish children have to face the hard fact that this is not *their* holiday—that the carolling and advertisements on television are addressed to someone else. Some accept this situation easily; some are filled with resentment; some (whose parents provide a Chanukah bush) are a bit confused.

My first child just didn't understand, as every child in the neighborhood but she had a gleaming bauble in the window.

"If we lived in a Jewish neighborhood . . ." I began.

"But we don't," said my husband.

Most of the neighbor's children were kind. They listened politely as I explained about Chanukah more for my child's benefit than for theirs. But there was one little demon who had to have his say.

"Hey, kid," he chirped loudly, "don't you know what day it is?"

I heard him through the window and pulled back the drape to watch.

My little girl just stood there and brushed the tears away with a snowy mitten.

"Please, God," I prayed, "help her."

"I forgot," he went on. "You don't believe in God."

"I do, I do," she screamed. "I do." She ran up the steps and pounded on the door. I ran out to her.

"Tell him, Mommy, tell him." My mind flooded with long-ago memories, long-ago hurts.

"Go home, little boy," I said. "Go home and tell your Mother what you said. And never come near my house again."

"Honey, he's a child," said my husband. "He has to learn."

"I know," I said. "I started his education."

Five minutes later his mother appeared at our door.

"I don't know what to say," she said. "He never heard that from us. I don't want you to think——"

"I don't think anything," I said. "It had to happen sometime. I guess I was only waiting for it."

She was surprised.

"That's right," said my husband. "Every Jew finds out sometime. It's just that she's only a little girl."

"Yes," I said. "That's why I scolded your son. Next time she'll do her own fighting."

Our little girl listened in silent dignity. She looked at the woman steadily.

"I do believe in God," she said. Perhaps it was at that moment she traded the tinsel and the glamor for her own birthright.

My second daughter had no trouble accepting her role. In fact she is willing to deliver theological lectures free-of-charge at any time. A question like, "What is Santa going to bring you, little girl?" can elicit an entire monologue on "Santa won't bring me anything because Jewish children don't believe in Santa Claus because they don't celebrate Christmas because——" She dampens the questioner's ardor a bit with her display of catechistical erudition, but she is a woman of principle and has been ever since she could talk.

Explanations, however, from her and from me have backed us into more than one corner. I remember a conversation with one of my gentile neighbors as I tried to explain why my children didn't have a Christmas tree. Explaining was like walking on eggs, a treacherous and socially disasterous experience. Despite my extreme care, I felt remarkably heavy-footed and very sure that I was doing well at losing friends and alienating people.

"It's silly," she said. "A tree is of no religious significance. I can't see why your children should be denied."

"Well," I said. "I believe in principle and since Jewish people never have trees, they might as well learn."

"Never? Why, I know some Jewish people——"

"They just don't live up to principle," I said virtuously.

We were interrupted by two voices directed at me.

"Hey, Mom," the voices said. "Hurry up, we have to help Aunt Mary decorate the tree."

"Oh," smiled the neighbor, sanctimoniously. "Oh—principle, indeed?" Nodding knowingly, she left, never waiting to hear that Aunt Mary was not a relative, but a gentile friend upon whom my children had conferred the honorary position of aunthood.

To get back to my eldest, however, we have had our ups-and-downs at the Yule season. During the Christmas of her eighth year, she was given a one-line part in the school's annual pageant. The rabbi had already advised against allowing our children to appear in such performances but since it was a class project, and since she was the only Jewish child in that class, and since her part was negligible, I didn't think it worth creating any dissension.

I listened to her rehearse, "Hail, the spirit of joy is near!" and watched her emote before her mirror. She was as skinny and scrawny as an eight-year-old could be, but the piping voice was loud and clear.

"She has remarkable delivery," I said to my husband.

"Too bad she hasn't anything much to deliver," he said, "but in this case, it's just as well."

The day of the performance arrived. Since she wasn't exactly overjoyed with her role, she didn't urge me to attend. I didn't press the matter since it would have meant my taking time off to be in the audience, and my own teaching chores were piled high.

On my way home, I stopped at the grocer's for a few items only to overhear . . .

"Do you know that little Jewish girl?"

"You mean the one that was the whole show? That's Anne B———. Her mother's a school teacher."

"A school teacher?"

The two women who were talking became aware of my presence.

"Oh, Mrs. B———," smiled one. "Your little girl was so wonderful. Such a performance!"

"Performance?" I said. "She only had——"

"Now don't be modest. She was the whole show. And what a Santa Claus she made!"

"Santa Claus! You must be talking about someone else."

I was confused as I drove to Anne's school to pick her up. She was standing at the door with the principal!

"Mrs. B———," he said, with a broad smile. "You missed a beautiful performance. Anne stole the show. What training you've given this child!"

"Mr. Lyons," I said. "I don't understand. This morning Anne had a one-line part and this afternoon she is a star. What happened?"

"That's show biz," he smiled coyly. "I should have called you, but I didn't realize you wouldn't be here. Well, it seems Duane, who was to be our Santa came down with the measles. His mother called early this morning. The teacher in charge of the pageant didn't know what to do, and in desperation she asked if one of the children might not know the part—just from listening to rehearsals."

"And Anne knew?"

"Every line. Our Anne saved the day."

Yes, our Anne—skinny little Anne in a Santa costume designed for roly-poly Duane came to the rescue and became a star. The only flaw in the story is that never will she be able to say when she becomes a great actress that she had her start in the Yiddish theatre.

# 23  Sister Bobbie

When Anne graduated from high school, there was among her gifts a small silver *chai* on a chain, a gift from a friend whose acquaintance she had made when she was a tenthgrader enrolled in a summer creative writing course in a nearby parochial school. She had been expertly conditioned by her contemporaries and well cautioned as to what she might expect from "the sisters." The first few days I heard nothing but complaints about the prayers that opened every class and about fellow students who inscribed JMJ in the corner of every manuscript, but suddenly, the complaints ceased. Everything was pie and honey, and I was happy that my little fish in strange waters was adjusting. I wasn't quite prepared for over-adjustment, but I wasn't really unprepared either; for after fifteen years, I knew my daughter was prone to sudden aberrations.

"Mom," she said, "I think I'm going to join a convent."

"A Jewish convent? You'll have trouble finding one."

"Then I'll start one—and we'll go off into the wilderness to convert the savages."

"Ummm."

"Mom—you're not interested." The voice was tearful and hurt.

I peered over my bifocals at my own dear Sarah Heartburn. This new decision meant one of two things—either her new coiffure was unsatisfactory after hours of torment or her current beloved had disappointed her. But I mustn't pry—that wasn't the way the game was played.

"My dear, I am always interested." I hoped I didn't sound as weary as I felt. "But you're not serious."

"Well, Sister Bobbie thinks I'm serious."

"Sister who?" I wasn't aware she knew any of her teachers so intimately.

"Sister Bobbie . . . that's what we call her . . . at least, that's what I call her . . . Bobbie for short, that is . . ."

"Short for what? Bobbie socks or bobby pins?"

"Oh, mother . . ."

"Don't 'oh, mother' me . . . how many times have I told you that I don't want you to be disrespectful."

"I'm not being disrespectful. Bobbie is short for Robertine."

"Oh . . ." Uncomfortably, I went back to the mending. "Well, it still sounds disrespectful."

"It isn't at all, Mother, it's a sign of my sincere affection."

"I hope Sister Bobbie, that is, Sister Robertine feels that way when she hears it. Sisters sometimes don't understand . . ."

"Oh, mother . . ." There was a long silence broken only by the crunch of Anne's apple and the occasional snip of my scissors.

"She's wonderful, Mother."

"Who?"

"Sister Bobbie . . . she's a real kook."

"Anne . . . you don't refer to a nun as a kook, real or otherwise."

"Mom, I only mean that she's keen . . . way out . . . human, sort of . . ."

"Oh . . ."

"Like the other day when we needed a ride out to Shaker High and we couldn't get anybody to take us and she stopped old Mister Bates . . ."

"*Old* Mister Bates? I'll have you know I went to school with Stanley Bates."

"I didn't mean old old . . . I mean he kind of acts old and mean-like."

"Well, he was always a little hard to get along with."

"That's what I was saying. Well, she just smiles and asks him for a ride for herself and for all of us and he smiles and says 'yes' and even comes back to pick us up."

"Maybe he's not so mean, after all . . ."

"That's not what Sister Bobbie said . . ."

"What did she say?"

"She said, 'Girls, with a sweet smile and a habit, you can ask for anything.' She even offered to loan it to us sometime. She was only kidding, of course."

"Of course," I echoed feebly.

Anne's first apple core thumped into the waste basket and she reached for a second Macintosh.

"But she is so wonderful to talk to, Mom. You know I asked her all about Sister Luke."

"Who is Sister Luke?"

"The nun in *The Nun's Story* . . . you know how I loved *The Nun's Story* . . . I read it about six times . . ."

"No, I didn't know."

"Well, I did; it was so wonderful how she went to the tropics to fight TB and everything . . ."

"Malaria, do you mean?"

"No, remember how Sister Luke got TB and she was so pale and glamorous and everything and she couldn't even let herself fall in love with the handsome doctor . . ."

"I should hope not."

"Oh, Mother . . ."

"Your version seems a little different from the one I read."

"Well, I suppose after six times, I started to read between the lines . . ."

"Ummm . . ."

"Well, anyway, Sister Bobbie says that being a nun is nothing like that . . . that the story was romanticized and not very accurate. She says that nuns are just like other people, that they don't even have to wear black pajamas."

"What?" I could feel my eyebrows rising. "How did you find out about a nun's pajamas?"

"Asked . . ."

"What did you ask?"

"Well, I asked if she wore black all the time, like when she went to bed and she said . . ."

"Anne I've known people who have gone to parochial grammar schools and Catholic high schools and Catholic colleges, but I never have known anyone who had the nerve to ask a nun what she wore to bed."

"Weren't they curious?"

"If they were, they kept it to themselves." My mind went back to stories I had heard from Catholic youngsters about black-robed mentors . . . about their discipline . . . their unapproachability . . . it would take someone like Anne . . . what was it about God taking care of fools and angels or was it something about fools rushing in where angels feared to tread . . .

"It was very interesting, Mom. She told us all about how a salesman comes to the convent and they pick out whatever they need in whatever size and color he has, or he gets them what they want. Sister Bobbie likes florals, she says . . . kind of a relief from all that black. She bought a blue bathing suit. I told her she should get a two-piece job like mine but she said that was a little too much."

"I should hope so."

"She swims a lot and skates, too . . . she says that she taught all her younger brothers and sisters . . . she's the oldest of six kids, you know."

"I suppose she told you about them, too."

"Oh, sure." Another apple core thumped into the basket. "We talk a lot at lunch."

"You eat lunch with the Sister?"

"Every day. Then I help correct papers in her room. Some days she brings sandwiches and some days I bring them. She likes everything but peanut butter and banana—together, I mean."

"Well, that's one passion you don't share. What do you bring?"

"Usually salami."

"Does Sister Bobbie like kosher salami? It is a trifle smelly."

"She loves it—especially with dill pickles."

I couldn't see how the woman could relish a salami sandwich on a hot July day but there's no accounting for tastes.

"Anne," I admonished, "I don't want you to make a pest of yourself."

"I don't, Mom, honest . . . it's just that she's so nice and so attractive. Her hands are like two birds, always fluttering around her veil. She says it gets in her way."

"Really?"

"Yes . . . it's the way she shakes her head . . . the pins all fly . . . but she showed me where she keeps her supply."

"Supply?"

"Well, she has to replace the ones she loses so she keeps extra pins under her collar. You know it lifts right up. And do you know that collar isn't cloth . . . it's just something they wipe off like plastic . . . she showed me how they pin it in place and everything . . ."

"She showed you?"

"Ummm . . ." Thump went another apple core.

"Because you asked her?"

"Ummm."

"Oh, Anne." My small groan died in a long silence that was broken too soon by another query.

"Mom, do nuns keep their heads shaved?"

"Anne, I don't know."

"I'll ask . . ."

"Anne, don't you dare ask another thing. I'll die if I ever have to meet Sister Bobbie, I mean, Robertine. What will she think of the way I've brought you up?"

"Oh, don't worry about that, Mom. She said she was going to call you . . ."

"Oh, no," I thought. "This is too much. She'll tell me I have a busy-body of a daughter who has no respect for a nun's position and that I should teach her to hold her tongue and mind her manners and . . ."

"Mom . . ."

"Yes, Anne?" In my daze, I thought I heard bells or at least, a bell.

"Telephone, Mom."

"Thank you, Anne . . . Oh, yes, Sister Bobbie, I mean, Sister Robertine, we were just talking about you . . . I must explain . . . apologize . . . Anne doesn't mean . . . oh, you think that Anne is a delightful child, so interested, so

vital . . . she does what? Oh, she brightens your day . . .
she's a pleasure to have around . . . well, thank you, Sister
Bobbie, I mean, Robertine . . . what? . . . You like Bobbie?
Because it makes you feel that the girls love you . . . Oh,
they do, Sister Bobbie, they do."

Anne watched me drop the phone back into its cradle.
She crunched another apple.

"Isn't she way out, Mom? Way out?"

"Oh, yes, Anne, she is . . . she is . . ."

# 24  At Random

When Mom and Pop were first married, they were dirt-poor, a situation not much improved by the arrival of their first born. But even the poor have toothaches and Mom was no exception. Grandma sent her to the family dentist and she went reluctantly, clutching her last two dollars. She was rather taken aback by the tall burly man who commanded her to "Open wide" because he certainly looked more muscular than dextrous.

"What's your name?"

She grunted an answer past his hairy hand.

"Oh, you're one of the Jews from the Dyke."

She nodded as much as she could nod her pinioned head.

"Funny thing about Jews. They all have money."

Mom thought about the two dollars in her shabby purse. It represented her total capital at the moment.

"Rich-rich-rich—" he sing-songed. "Tell me, why are all Jews rich?"

He took his hand out of her mouth so she could answer.

"When you finish, Doctor, I'll tell you," said Mom, with the canniness of a Scheherazade.

He resumed his task with all the finesse of a karate expert and soon waved an eroded bicuspid in her face.

"There it is," he crowed, as Mom opened her purse to get out her money.

"Hey," he said, "you promised to tell me why you Jews are all so rich."

"Well, doctor," Mom began. "It's really very simple. Jesus was a Jew and he likes to bless the poor, and because there are so many poor, it's hard to make a choice—but He had to choose. So what can He do? He chooses His own—because, after all, you know and I know—blood is thicker than water."

When I first entered college, I was introduced to a department head who was slightly deaf.

"What's your name?" she asked.

"Newell," I answered.

"Newman! How nice!" she responded. "Any relation to the Cardinal?"

Somehow she never did get my negative response and any number of people knew me as the Jewish girl who was a Cardinal's niece.

I was born on Saint Patrick's Day but I escaped being named Patricia because an Irish neighbor lady had had a girl baby the year previous and named her Miriam. Mom loved the name and tagged me with it. That's one way for a Jew to get a Hebrew name.

A friend of mine is a defensive Jew, always ready to do battle for a cause and a little deflated when there is no cause. We were having breakfast in a diner, and she was growing indignant every time she heard the counterman make some reference to "two Jews."

"Once more," she steamed, "and I'm going to tell him

off. Who does he think he is? This is a public place and I don't have to sit here and take his insults."

"Calm yourself," I said. "It's no insult to be called a Jew. You're one and I'm one and that makes two."

"You and your sense of humor! It's not funny. Let's pay him and get out of here."

"As soon as I finish my coffee."

While I sipped, she glared. Then we went up to the counter to pay the anti-Semite, only to break up with laughter as our auditory organs began to function.

"Two juice," he was chanting into the counter microphone for the man in the back room.

A Negro editor reprimanded me for using the word "Negress." Bad form, he told me. I hadn't known but it gave me food for thought. Why is "Jewess" considered acceptable? Isn't it just as ridiculous? We haven't concocted anything like Catholicess or Protestantess or Seventh Day Adventess.

"Mom," said my daughter, mulling over the proper way to refuse a gentile boy a date, "it's not my image I'm worried about—it's the image of my people."

When I asked my eight-year-old why she didn't want to tell her gentile classmates about *Chanukah,* she responded, "They know I'm Jewish. Must I make an issue of it?"

Our local YWCA was giving a benefit dinner and several of us informed the lady in charge that ham steak was taboo, but that we would enjoy fish.

"Don't worry," she said, "you'll have a delicious dinner. I'll order lobster newburg for all of you."

"It's really more expensive when a Protestant dies," said one of my colleagues discussing the outlay of our faculty fund. "After all, you can get a mass card for as little as a dollar."

My husband's back troubled him so he decided to visit a physician up the block. Without examining him, the doctor tallied his symptoms and announced, "It's the same with a lot of the fellows of your generation. You need to be circumcised."

My husband couldn't restrain his laughter.

"It's not funny," said the doctor. "It can be very painful."

"I imagine it can, doc. I really should know, but I don't remember. You see, you're forty years too late."

"Hey, Miriam, do you know Barney Greenfield from East Podunk? He's Jewish, too."

At last count, there were six million Jews in the United States and I'm supposed to know all of them intimately.

"It's your fault she doesn't believe in Heaven or Hell," challenged one friend, blaming me for the heresy of another.

"What makes you think I don't believe in them?" I replied. "After all, they were invented by and for Jews."

My friend who lived through a German concentration camp has still retained his sense of humor.

"The first people on the moon will be Jews," he said. "After all, that's one place we haven't escaped to yet."

My mother read the account of Goldwater's speech to the Polish-American brotherhood.

"Your grandfathers and mine came from the same place," he sentimentalized, "and we share a common European heritage."

"He should mention who was chasing who," she sputtered. "All they shared was a pitchfork and his grandfather was on the wrong end."

"Norman Mailer helped me to rid himself of a sense of guilt," says a prominent black writer. It might be interesting to find out who the Spaniard or German or Pole was who helped Mailer for such selfish reasons.

I invited a representative of Blue Cross to speak to a group where I was employed. The man's name was Patrick Xavier O'Brien, but I overheard the comment, "Just like a Jew—trying to get business for one of their own."

Until the day comes when I refrain from using such terms as "wop" or "polack" or "nigger," I have no right to resent "kike."

"Mom," says my eight-year-old. "I know Tony's not Jewish, but it really isn't anything serious."

When I asked the waiter in a kosher restaurant for iced tea, he turned to my husband with, "Why do you bring a *shiksa* to a place like this?"

My totally gentile English class loved reading "Fiddler on the Roof" and even began to appreciate some of the implications of anti-Semitism. *Mazel Tov* was never said with more aplomb and enthusiasm; and a *Mazel Tov* to them and good health and more understanding.

Pop's mother insisted on her family's speaking English as soon as they docked on American shores. As a result, her children spoke the language with the same lack of skill with which most natives are endowed. At first, this presented some difficulties because there are times and places when quick translation was hard to come by.

There was a time when Grandpa was fixing the roof of a little house he had rented for his brood in a place called Willow Glen. His pants caught on the metal and he hung suspended. He yelled down to the *landsman* who was helping him, "Yussel, look in the book and see how you say *'G'vald'* in America." Yussel reached for the book but before he could find the proper entry, Grandpa's pants gave, and there was need for little but first aid and horse liniment.

Grandma, too, had her troubles. She had acquired a chicken which laid her one egg a day. Fresh eggs were hard to get so she decided to acquire herself a flock large enough to supply her family's needs. Without further ado, she dressed herself properly in her suit and sailor hat and proceeded to a poultry market uptown. In her very best English, she explained her needs, several pullets and a "gentleman from the chickens." The store keeper opened the trap door to his basement, went down and soon returned with a beautiful rooster in hand.

"Here you are, lady," he said. "He's just what you want, but he ain't no gentleman."

Received a form letter from a magazine asking for entries to the poetry contest. Since my file is full of miscellaneous efforts, I forwarded three of same. Weeks later, my mail contained a copy of this magazine of evangelical persuasion, and as I thumbed through, I found my name among the contest winners. Also listed were the rules for the contest, first of which was that the poet must be Christian. I then sat down at my typewriter to dash off a hot note to the editor withdrawing my entry and using an old tried-and-true reprimand, informed him that "Any contest that would exclude the work of Jesus Christ can also exclude mine." I hoped that the least my gesture would accomplish was to embarrass the editor, but I didn't even manage that. The editor promptly returned my poem, thanked me for my frankness and said that he would pray for the day when I should see the light.

Editors are an odd bunch. The managing head of a Jewish publication rejected a children's story dealing with the life of Emma Lazarus on the grounds that I emphasized Judaism too much. The editor of a Methodist publication accepted the same story but asked why I didn't stress Miss Lazarus's religious background more.

My brother Manny is really schizoid . . . on the one hand he complains about all the Jews in Miami but on the other hand he is very impressed with the big temple they've named after him.

Recently we moved from a home in which we had lived for about twelve years and a gentile friend remarked that our decision to go was probably prompted by a desire to live in a Jewish neighborhood. And that may have had something to do with our decision although I was surprised to learn that my new neighbors, the Clancys and the Ryans and the O'Toole's, were M.O.T. (Members of the Tribe) .

Moving to a new home is an auspicious occasion, one we felt would be incomplete without the proper religious ritual. Since our rabbi graciously makes it his custom to personally supervise the hanging of the *mezuzah,* I phoned and we made the arrangements for a convenient hour. The appointed evening was warm and I decided to relax on the front porch until he arrived. A neighbor chanced along and joined us for a moment of conversation. When I told him of our plans for the evening, he simply shook his head and said, "Well, I hope you have better luck than we had with the priest from St. Xavier's. He promised to bless our house a year ago and he hasn't been here yet." I assured him that our rabbi was the soul of promptness and had never been known to forget an appointment. "I hope so," he answered, gloomily unconvinced.

Soon his sister joined us and I repeated my story. I explained the significance of the *mezuzah,* its relationship to the first commandment, and quoted the phrase "and ye shall inscribe it on your doorposts" for further clarity. They nodded and we waited. Eight o'clock came . . . then nine . . . then ten . . . and finally eleven. Our friends rose to leave.

"Same thing happened to us," she said.

"Yeah," he said, "but at least they can hang their own moose."

We had the loveliest time at the Donovan's twenty-fifth anniversary party. We discussed *The Dead Sea Scrolls* with John, Junior, who is studying for the priesthood and showed him the correct tempo for *Hava Nagila.* His beginner's Hebrew is a little rusty, but he can play a way-out *Hatikvah* on the organ followed by an encore of *My Wild Irish Rose.*

Child rearing is an occupation plagued by doubts. We arrive at certain concepts of right and wrong, and then we wonder whether we have the right to foist our conclusions upon our young.

Because I come from an immigrant background of European persecution and hatred, and because I am a teacher of American history, I want my children to sense the wonder of America. I want them to love the ideals upon which this great land was built, and to appreciate how much the strength of this country depends upon the attitudes of each individual. Most of all, I want them to understand and respect the needs of their fellow Americans and not to have that understanding eroded by the petty prejudices to which we are all victim.

The town we lived in is small. Its views are provincial. Its prejudices are inalienable, passed down from one generation to another as part of family folklore.

There is danger in teaching broadmindedness in such a climate. I was asking my children to wage war on established attitudes, perhaps in so doing to forego their own acceptance and comfort. Did I have the right? Would my children suffer by being markedly different? A difference, even in attitude, may lead to penalties a child may not be ready or willing to pay.

"You have to be taught to hate," Oscar Hammerstein wrote, and I had to be sure that my children did not learn. I had to administer the antitoxin for one of the most dreaded viruses of all mankind—intolerance. I was not at all sure that the preventative measures might not be as deadly in results as the disease.

With that in mind, such traditional nursery fodder as "eeney, meeney, miney, mo" was amended to "catch a bunny by the toe." No one seemed to care. *Little Black Sambo* was assigned to the garbage pail, and no one missed him. Words like "nigger," "kike," and "wop" were assigned to the *bad* list. We refrained from them as we would if the words had been profanity.

Discussions of religious problems were aired openly, pro and con. My neighbors, I am sure, doubted both my sense and my patriotism; but my neighbors were not my main concern. If I had prejudices, I no longer defended them. If I did *not* possess a particular prejudice, I freely confessed my motive—personal cowardice—in not taking positive action. If I did not at all times stand with right, I admitted my own lack in doing nothing.

But how does one measure attitude? Can you ever tell how much a child has learned? I was not sure. I did know that my children were more at ease with the world and more at ease in expressing a contradictory opinion than I ever was.

I remember that as a child I insulted my aunt's cook by calling her "Aunt Jemima." I did not know why this name angered her, and as much as I loved her, I couldn't ask. All I could do was beg pardon. A discussion was out of the question.

For that reason, I worried as I heard my daughter talking to the carpenter who worked for us!

"Mister Barton, why are you colored and I am white?" asked my eight-year-old.

"Because we had different daddies, honey," he laughed.

"It could be the other way around, couldn't it?"

"Sure could."

"Would you mind?"

"Guess not. Might make life easier; but if I didn't have my troubles, there'd be others. That's the way things are."

The child shrugged and went back to her playing. Later I overheard her in conversation with a neighbor.

"Does that colored man work for you, Anne?" the woman asked.

"Colored man? Oh, you mean Mister Barton?" Something in the way she answered was a reprimand, and I smiled to myself.

Shortly thereafter, he came to the house with his little girl, who was attired in a brand new Annie Oakley outfit, a red cowgirl hat on her black braids. My four-year-old stared in wonder. Knowing that Debby had never seen a colored child, I held my breath for fear of what she might say.

"Mommy, Mommy!" she blurted out.

"What, honey?" I answered patiently and carefully.

"Mommy, will you ask that little girl where she got her hat? I want one just like that!"

Then I knew. Understanding is a gift children are born with. Their vision is clear. It only becomes clouded and contaminated by the animosities and hatreds they acquire from adults around them.*

---

* Reprinted from *Home Life.*

# 25  I'm a Judeophile

People like to collect things—match box covers, bottle caps, stamps, coins—so I collect Jews. It's become a kind of passion to identify those who are and those who aren't. The image-makers tend to lump all Jews together—"All Jews are rich," "All Jews are Communists," "All Jews are brilliant"—one could go on *ad nauseum* with the generalizations defining what Jews are. Jews themselves generalize, thereby adding to the sum total of stereotypes which exist.

Intellectually, I know better; but emotionally, I am none too bright. Since I am an American history buff, I have, by some coincidence, amassed more than a few details concerning such men as Asser Levy, Haym Soloman and Judah Benjamin. I have ferreted out the fact that most of the thirteenth-century traders who took the overland routes to Asia in search of spices were of our breed, and, in my heart of hearts, I accept the theory that brings Columbus into our fold.

I revel in the accounts of the life of Benjamin Disraeli even though I know he was a lifelong convert to Christianity; but what he does for my pride is wonderful. It's as if his tactical skill and political acumen were things I could be personally proud of; as if he were a member of my own family. How many times I have relived that wonderful scene when he rose in the House of Lords to answer the insults of some of his peers and thundered:

"Gentlemen, my ancestors were writing poetry in the halls of Zion when yours were eating each other."

*Touché!* Score! One for our side!

Over the years, I have developed a kind of sureness that I have some built-in device that would aid me in identifying any Jew on first sight. Time was to prove that I was about as accurate as the Nazis were when they selected Leslie Howard as their example of the pure Aryan type. Leslie, blonde, blue-eyed, cool beautiful example of British masculine pulchritude was slightly Hebraic.

My worst lesson came when my husband took me car-buying. He introduced me to the short, stout salesman whose friendly face was framed by kinky sandy-colored curls and whose smile widened to make his overwhelming nose seem more convex.

"Honey, Sam and I went to school together," my spouse explained.

"*Vus mackst eer?*" I chirped, which means "How are you?" in my pidgin Yiddish.

Sam's smile stayed broad.

"He's fine, honey," answered my husband, giving me an elbow.

I moved away from the nudge, totally unconscious of its intent.

"This is the car we like," said Sam, pointing to a pink and black hard top.

"Wow! That's a real *meeiskeit*" I said, indicating my displeasure. "I like this one," I said, indicating a beige convertible.

Sam raised his eyebrows and my husband shrugged.

"It's more money," said Sam.

"*Veef'l?*" I questioned.

Sam cupped his hand to his ear as if he didn't hear well. This time, I didn't get out of the way of the nudge fast enough and collected a black and blue rib. Friend husband then grabbed my elbow and steered me out.

"Sam," he said, "we'll be back next week sometime. I just remembered an appointment I have to keep."

"What's your hurry?" I sputtered as we were out of earshot. "I thought we were buying a car."

"Not til you learn to speak English."

"You've got a nerve. I can speak English."

"So why don't you? That fellow thought you were crazy."

"But you said——"

"I said we went to school, together not *cheder*."

"But he looks——"

"He looks nothing——"

"He's not Jewish?"

"Not so's you'd notice it. His name is Sam Chalakis and I think he's part Greek and part Irish."

"Oh-no." My groan was more than from embarrassment; it was also from learning that my Judeo-detecting device was malfunctioning.

Over the years, I have often looked around our synagogue on the High Holy Days and say to myself, "If I saw Mr. X or Mrs. Y somewhere else, would I know? Would I be sure those dark exotic children over there were not Assyrian or Armenian? Would I be sure those little blondes were not French or German?" The more I look, the more unsure I become, and the more I learn how little externals mean.

Recently, at a Bar Mitzvah, I sat near a shawl-wrapped gentleman who was absorbed in reading his prayer book. With his *yamulka* set back on his head, he was the picture of a devout Jew.

"Who's he?" I said to the woman next to me.

"I don't know. He's very familiar; but I can't tell you who he is."

"He doesn't belong to this temple?"

"No, I'm sure he doesn't."

Again and again, my eyes were drawn to the man but recognition did not come. After the service, he folded the shawl, removed the yamulka and turned to leave. As he passed me, I spoke without even thinking."

"Why, Tom," I said, "what are you doing here?" I knew the man—he was the teller in a local bank and decidedly not Jewish.

"What are you doing here?" I asked.

"Oh, the Cohens are old friends, and I wouldn't have missed Ronnie's *Bar Mitzvah* for the world."

"You didn't seem lost during the service. Is this your first one?"

"No," he said. "During the war, the army discovered that I was an Episcopal rector and they made me chaplain's assistant. Our chaplain happened to be a rabbi, and by the end of the war, I had presided at enough services not to feel ill at ease with any of them."

"That's very interesting," I said, embarrassed that I had cross-questioned him.

He smiled. "Now," he said, "will you join me for the *kiddush*?"

# Epilogue:
# My Life Among the Gentiles*

For over two decades, I have taught school in a small city in upstate New York. During most of the time, I have been the only Jewish member of the faculty. Others were hired from time to time, but until recently, few became an integral part of the educational set-up. This was actually their choice not that of the administration, but whatever the reasons, I was a lone representative. I have had my share of ups and downs with faculty members, students, and other personnel, but for the most part, I have always felt a part of the world I lived in: not segregated or tolerated, but a real part of my own little society.

I grew up in this same little city with its population of some 23,000 gentiles and possibly 130 Jews. I went to grade school there and high school there and then commuted to a nearby institution of higher learning. I had dreamed for many years of going to college, to a place that would be filled with fun and fellowship à la the

---

* This article was originally printed in *Jewish Frontier*.

movies. With my Anglican name and non-stereotyped
face, it was my misfortune to be readily accepted. For
about a month, I was rushed by the most desirable and
influential sorority on campus. They could and did prom-
ise me everything until they found out the "truth." To
their credit, I will say that they were sheepish as they with-
drew the hand of sisterhood and explained carefully all
about the rigidity and holiness of their by-laws. And they
did invite me quite cordially to feel free to come to the
house at any time; I would always be a welcome guest.
There was a certain amount of irony in their honesty;
they never considered for a moment that I wouldn't understand. After all, my situation wasn't unusual—only my
naïveté.

There were others like me, some in even worse situations. There were the Jewish boys who were taken by twos
and threes in a sort of quota arrangement into the largest
house on campus. Elated at their acceptance, they soon
found themselves ostracized by the rest of the Jewish fellows. Some would have turned down the bids had they
realized the situation, but others who were taken into
membership refused to recognize that a not-so-gentlemanly
arrangement even existed. There was one lad, a convert
to Christian Science, who spent four unhappy years pointing out his non-Jewishness, only to be constantly identified
by his own fraternity brothers as their "Jewish member."
He was living evidence of their broad-mindedness. There
was the devout Catholic girl whose possibly Jewish surname gave the sorority sleuths the idea that the girl's father might be Jewish, also. He was, and so the Catholic
sororities considered her a Jew while the Jewish sororities
regarded her a Catholic. Being neither fish nor fowl, she
was simply cast off into a limbo of loneliness.

It was at this time that I began to tilt windmills; to wage small battles against an attitude I did not understand. I deliberately snared myself a few gentile beaux so that I could attend parties and dances that otherwise would have been inaccessible to me. I took pleasure in "crossing the color line" and felt a sweet satisfaction in knowing that my presence was annoying to some. I proudly attended the St. Patrick's Day frolic with the president of Newman Club and thrilled to every note as the band played a "Happy Birthday" just for me. I attended dance after dance at a fraternity which preferred to disband rather than accept a few college regulations broadening their admissions policies for rushees. To this day, I am not sure of what I was proving other than my acceptability as a human being. The time came when I was convinced that the activities on one side of the fence were identical with the activities on the other, and it was at this point that I was more than content to go back with "my own kind."

Getting a teaching job twenty-five years ago wasn't easy for anyone, and it was doubly difficult for those in minority groups. I was turned down in little towns that God had forgotten when my interviewer discovered I couldn't teach Sunday School. Jewish students changed their names, covered up tell-tale affiliations, answered personnel questions vaguely, all in an attempt to get a job. After a half-dozen unsuccessful interviews, I went to my supervisor for help. She had already written a glowing recommendation, but I hoped she could offer some kind of lead. She shook her head sadly; she had only one suggestion—perhaps I might like working in a department store.

It was in my own home town I found a job. I was qualified; I was competent; they needed teachers; but I received my appointment through political influence. The crusty old politician who ran the place liked my dad and he had promised to see that I was placed as soon as I finished college. I am idealistic enough to wish that it hadn't had to happen that way, but I am honest enough to admit that it did. I am also grateful for the fact that I have lived long enough to see jobs begging for teachers and not teachers begging for jobs. That same old man taught me another lesson, too. He wasn't an educated man like the scholarly fellows who managed the back-woods education of the state; he didn't have a B.A. or an M.A. in educational psychology; he couldn't read or write. He certainly couldn't be classified as a pillar of the community and he couldn't abide upstanding citizens. He had seen too many of them with their hats in their hands. But he had one quality the others lacked; he didn't care whether a person was polka-dotted or striped, a church-goer or a church-stayer-awayer. He filled jobs for his own reasons and at his own whim and gathered together as fine a group as one could find in any area, even one where selection was made by approved methods.

Teaching has been a series of learning experiences for me. As I had to cope with the situations that we all, Jew and gentile, have to face, I have learned not to go into instant shock if someone tactlessly offends me. I don't let it pass, but neither do I become emotionally scarred. I have come to believe that people deserve to be embarrassed by their ignorance. Recently, a salesman was trying to sell us an expensive movie projector, and I told him frankly that I would like to buy it but that it might be hard to convince the school board to spend so much money.

"Just be like the Jewish merchants," he said. "They can always cry to make a sale."

The two teachers standing with me were obviously embarrassed, but I was determined to see how well he could extricate his foot from his mouth.

"I guess I qualify on religious grounds," I said, "but since you're the salesman, you'd better do your own crying to the board."

With that, I left and he followed to apologize and to add that he hoped his "slip" wouldn't influence my decision. "After all," he said, "I didn't know you were Jewish."

"No, you didn't," I agreed. "Perhaps you should check these small details. I don't know what you are, either, but I couldn't care less."

He hovered over me for a while and then left. I hope he learned to curb his little jokes; I have little tolerance for "his kind."

There have been many times that I wished that I were someone else somewhere else, but then I know that perhaps it is good that I am just where I am. As a history teacher, I have brought details to my class that others might not have given them. My classes learned that good Queen Isabella, the patron of Columbus, was not so good. They learned a bit about her part in the Inquisition, about her quaint custom of confiscating the property of those she had condemned to death by fire and about her generosity in giving Columbus jewels that were not hers. I have explained to them why most of the caravan traders to China were Jewish and how the Jews of Europe were forced into usury. I have also brought up the question few history books ask, the question of where the so-called usurers obtained the money to lend. They had to get their stake from someone, and only kings and churchmen were that wealthy.

There were lots of other tales to be told also, from the accounts of the *pogroms* in Czarist Russia to the details of the Nazi terror. World War II was in progress, and a class discussion of rationing could prompt a remark like "the Jew merchants want it to drive up the prices." I am not sure that my explanation changed any minds, but at least I was there to administer a small dose of anti-toxin.

I also heard the "Maybe Hitler is right" statement from some of my students, and I had no compunction in asking these few, "How would you like my hide for a lampshade?" Shocking question to ask a child, but shock is acceptable therapy.

Christmas would inevitably bring some attack on the few Jewish children in the group. "Do you know that Myra never had a Christmas tree?", "Did you hear Sam say he doesn't believe in Christ?" and the perennial favorite, "Do you know that the Jews killed Christ?" The lone child tried to answer the charges hurled against him, and it is then that I, their teacher, could explain that I was of the same faith as Sam or Myra, and so, for that matter, was Jesus Christ. I also tried to make them understand that their own intolerance is defilement of the very day they celebrate.

At first, I was most sensitive to insults to "my own," but as time passed, I became acutely attuned to jibes at others. Words like "Wop" and "Polack" and "nigger" are taboo in my classroom; and snide remarks about "dumb Canucks" or "dirty Hunkies" can draw as much ire as profanity or other infractions of behavior.

With children, there can be anger, but with adults, the situation changes. Strong emotion is not practicable with people one must face day after day. There are times, however, when reaction is unavoidable. I remember one day, at luncheon, a group of us were discussing a little boy who was rapidly becoming a behavior problem. He happened to be of Italian descent. Each of us offered some opinion until one teacher said, "You know how hot-tempered all Italians are. What can we expect?" She blissfully ignored the fact that across from her sat a teacher, also of Italian descent, one of the sweetest and most stable people in the world.

Heedlessly, she plunged ahead. "After all, certain nationalities have certain characteristics, don't you think?" As Grand Poobah of the Rash Assumption Society, she probably meant her question to be rhetorical, but I was already burning on a short fuse. She wasn't one of my favorite people, anyway, I must admit. She constantly told me she was "Half-Jewish and half-Irish," but I had noted that she was inordinately proud of the latter and a trifle apologetic about the former.

"I really don't see the connection between disposition and geography," I responded.

"Look at me," she persisted. "I have a real Irish temper!"

"Well," I countered, "No one could accuse you of having a real Jewish head." She laughed, but not too heartily, and we're still friends, I guess; as good friends as we could ever be.

My students always had the best Christmas parties, and again, it may be that I was proving something, or it may be that I just like parties and fun. I know all about the separation of church and state, but I also know that in a poor town these festivities may be all that some children have, and I am not sure I would accomplish anything by an adamant stand. It is always their party—my gentile charges' party—not mine. I would like to ask Leonard

Bernstein if he feels any less a Jew when he gives a Christmas concert. Would the situation be affected in any way if he didn't? I don't know. Despite all the objections to Christmas celebrations in the public schools, I am sure they will continue. And I am sure that all the emotions that children feel at this time of the year are worth-while and uplifting. I remember one class that tried so hard to do the right thing; they gave me a Chanukah gift with a beautiful Chanukah card inside. The Christmas wrappings were just force of habit, and I have always enjoyed *White Christmas.* Of course, they had the whole situation topsy-turvy; of course, they didn't know the meaning of *Chanukah;* but they had accepted the fact that their teacher was different from them and that her customs were different from theirs. As a teacher, I am pleased at their learning that much. I am not a clergyman, I am not a legal expert, I am a teacher; and I know that learning is a long, slow, arduous, never-ending process. Unfortunately, this same process is the only solution to the problems involved with man's misunderstanding of man.

I have many Jewish friends who have moved from metropolitan areas into small towns which are either predominantly Catholic or predominantly Protestant. In both cases, they have found intolerance and have blamed it, *in toto,* on the group into whose midst they have fallen. In my years of living, I have found very little difference between an intolerant Protestant and an intolerant Catholic. Perhaps, the only one is that usually a Catholic will engage in a heated argument with you while a Protestant will not deign to do so. The Catholic is far more emotional because he is closer to memories of personal hurt. The intolerant Jew, however, for me, is the hardest to take, because he is the most stupid of the stupid. He has had the hardest lessons and has learned the least. As I move from Jewish group to gentile group, I find that I cannot turn completely chameleon and accept all the drivel I hear. I am uncomfortable explaining or defending one group to another, and I know that it is not my personal responsibility, but I refuse to walk away from misguided opinion. The voice of common sense is too often drowned out by the senseless and the violently vocal.

In more recent years, I have been teaching English literature, and as I read my youngsters' compositions, I see how they mirror my opinions. We discuss the mighty Caesar and the less-mighty Romans; we catalogue his virtues and his faults. We analyze Brutus and Cassius and again, the part of the people. Consciously or unconsciously, I lead them through a study of dictators, through cause and effect of the downfall of democracy. We read *Silas Marner* and I ask their reasons for his being a victim of intolerance and their analysis of the type of thinking which breeds this attitude. Here and there a thought or a sentence shows me I have left my mark and I am pleased. I no longer avoid taking sides on issues for I know that if a teacher sees the right, she cannot ignore it; if she sees a wrong, she cannot defend it. This does not mean that my classroom is a sounding board for all causes, because being a good "Yiddishe Mama," I place academic responsibility before academic freedom. The merits of cooperative citizenship, we discuss; the merits of drug addiction I leave for the great unwashed.

I have been naïve. There was a time I would argue that a high-school child should be allowed to read anything. Of course, that was before we had so many novels based on the boy meets boy theme. But I did remember my own teacher reading *The Merchant of Venice,* and she presented Shylock as a human being, a man who had been badgered beyond endurance, but who when he imitated the ways of his enemies, lost everything. I assumed that every educated person, every teacher, would have to interpret the story this way. I did not realize the harm that could be done until I inherited the class of a teacher who had done a vastly different job. This group told me about the "funny story of an old rat of a Jew who got what he deserved." I was shocked by the attitude of children who knew so few Jews and even more shocked by their teacher. The idea that an educated person can be small-minded is hard to accept for anyone brought up in the Jewish tradition of respect for the learned.

But a B.A. or an M.A. or even a Ph.D. doesn't make a *mensch.* I remember one of my college professors in sociology. He was a fat, blubbery, bald little man who became terribly upset if anyone happened to address him as "Mister" instead of "Doctor," and yet he called every nun in his classes "Miss." He complained about the "pushy little Jews" who were always trying for high grades, and we wondered how many he down-graded. Once, when asked a question about slavery, he answered that he didn't think "niggers" were worth discussing. This in the face of several colored students in the class.

I haven't known many teachers like this but I have known some who are less outspoken. In fact, they say little, they commit no overt act, but the feeling is there. They do their damage subtly and silently—and they are unforgivable when they attack children. There are those who run school publications and place some of the best Jewish creative talent in charge of advertising because "they're so good at that sort of thing." They are those

who give monthly tests on the high holy days and refuse
to let a youngster make up the grade. They are the ones
who senselessly insist that a Jewish child write a composi-
tion on "What Easter means to me." They are the ones
who ask me each year whether I get paid for the Jewish
holidays (I do!) but have yet to offer me the felicitations
of the season. They are the ones who regard me as some
kind of misguided heathen and I take pleasure in remind-
ing them that Jesus was one of "us."

But there are better things to remember also. There
are the students and teachers who never forget to send me
a *Rosh Hashonah* card; the gentile friends who send my
children *Chanukah* gifts and our family wine for Passover. There are those who return my *"Sholem"* with another *"Sholem"* and those I have taught to say *"l'chaim"*
with their cocktail. And I have learned that on St. Patrick's Day that when an Irish friend chants, "The top of
the morning to you," the proper response is "And the rest
of the day to you." And why not? To teach is to learn.

Several years ago, when an upsurge of Nazi smearings
ran rampant through America, my heart was heavy. I felt
that no one around me could possibly understand. But
early one morning, as we arose to salute the flag, my principal, who leads the ceremony, began by saying, "For one
moment, let us all, Christians and Jews, pause to pray for
a world where every man may live in dignity and safety,
a world where those indoctrinated with hate will never
control our lives and our destiny." Her words eased some
of my fears, and later, when I tried to thank her, she only
laughed and said, "You know this is my world, too."

There is an old saying that the more things change, the more they stay the same. Here I am, an octogenarian, and stuff still happens.

Recently, as a dinner guest at an assisted living facility, I was reintroduced to a resident who was from my old home town. I remembered her as a former school mate, in high school and college, and recalled one specific incident from my college freshman days. I was being rushed by the two "big" sororities, and unaware of certain restrictions, I was leaning toward the one favored by my two other Gentile high school pals. Then, I was told not to expect that bid because an old high school acquaintance, this same lady, had revealed my Jewish identity. I was momentarily shocked and hurt, but it was for the best. My chosen sorority had better exam files, better tutorials and best of all, it was there I met my beloved husband who didn't date "shikas." I owed the lady a big "thank you." However, to my amazement, she later stopped by our table and asked, "Which sorority did you belong to?"...my answer, "Not yours, honey."

Breinigsville, PA USA
10 March 2010
233896BV00001B/13/P